AF541264

HANDBOOK OF HORTICULTURAL SCIENCE

HANDBOOK OF HORTICULTURAL SCIENCE

By

Dr. H. Shivanna

Professor & Head

Deptt. of Forest Biology & Tree Improvement

College of Forestry

SIRSI, Uttar Kannada

Karnataka

(India)

DISCOVERY PUBLISHING HOUSE PVT. LTD.

NEW DELHI-110 002

First Published - 2012

Reprinted - 2016

ISBN: 978-93-5056-095-2

© Author

Handbook of Horticultural Science

Published by:

DISCOVERY PUBLISHING HOUSE PVT. LTD.
4383/4B, Ansari Road, Darya Ganj
New Delhi-110 002 (India)
Phone: +91-11-23279245, 43596064-65
Fax: +91-11-23253475
E-mail: discoverypublishinghouse@gmail.com
sales@discoverypublishinggroup.com
web: www.discoverypublishinggroup.com

Printed at:
Infinity Imaging Systems
Delhi

Preface

Horticulture is the industry and science of plant cultivation including the process of preparing soil for the planting of seeds, tubers, or cuttings. Horticulturists work and conduct research in the disciplines of plant propagation and cultivation, crop production, plant breeding and genetic engineering, plant biochemistry, and plant physiology. The work particularly involves fruits, berries, nuts, vegetables, flowers, trees, shrubs, and turf. Horticulturists work to improve crop yield, quality, nutritional value, and resistance to insects, diseases, and environmental stresses. Horticulture usually refers to gardening on a smaller scale, while agriculture refers to the large-scale cultivation of crops. The word is composite, from two words, horti, meaning grass, originating in the Greek, meaning the same (grass) and the word culture.

Horticulturists can work in industry, government or educational institutions or private collections. They can be cropping systems engineers, wholesale or retail business managers, propagators and tissue culture specialists (fruits, vegetables, ornamentals, and turf), crop inspectors, crop production advisers, extension specialists, plant breeders, research scientists, and of course, teachers.

Disciplines which complement horticulture include biology, botany, entomology, chemistry, mathematics, genetics, physiology, statistics, computer science, and communications, garden design, planting design. Plant science and horticulture courses include: plant materials, plant propagation, tissue culture, crop production, post-harvest handling, plant breeding, pollination management, crop nutrition, entomology, plant pathology, economics, and business. Some careers in horticultural science require a masters (MS) or doctoral (PhD) degree.

Horticulture is practiced in many gardens, “plant growth centres” and nurseries. Activities in nurseries range from preparing seeds and cuttings to growing fully mature plants.

Horticulture has a very long history. The study and science of horticulture dates all the way back to the times of Alexander the Great, and has been going on ever since, with present day horticulturists such as Freeman S. Howlett, the revolutionary horticulturist. The origins of horticulture lie in the transition of human communities from nomadic hunter-gatherers to sedentary or semi-sedentary horticultural communities, cultivating a variety of crops on a small scale around their dwellings or in specialized plots visited occasionally during migrations from one area to the next. (such as the ‘milpa’ or maize field of Mesoamerican cultures). In forest areas such horticulture is often carried out in swiddens (‘slash and burn’ areas). A characteristic of horticultural communities is that useful trees are often to be found planted around communities or specially retained from the natural ecosystem.

Author

Contents

Introduction

Horticulture is the industry and science of plant cultivation including the process of preparing soil for the planting of seeds, tubers, or cuttings. Horticulturists work and conduct research in the disciplines of plant propagation and cultivation, crop production, plant breeding and genetic engineering, plant biochemistry, and plant physiology. The work particularly involves fruits, berries, nuts, vegetables, flowers, trees, shrubs, and turf. Horticulturists work to improve crop yield, quality, nutritional value, and resistance to insects, diseases, and environmental stresses. Horticulture usually refers to gardening on a smaller scale, while agriculture refers to the large-scale cultivation of crops. The word is composite, from two words, horti, meaning grass, originating in the Greek, meaning the same (grass) and the word culture.

The Study of Horticulture

Horticulture involves eight areas of study, which can be grouped into two broad sections — ornamentals and edibles:

- Arboriculture is the study of, and the selection, planting, care, and removal of, individual trees, shrubs, vines, and other perennial woody plants.

- Floriculture includes the production and marketing of floral crops.
- Landscape horticulture includes the production, marketing and maintenance of landscape plants.
- Olericulture includes the production and marketing of vegetables.
- Pomology includes the production and marketing of fruits.
- Viticulture includes the production and marketing of grapes.

Postharvest physiology involves maintaining the quality of and preventing the spoilage of horticultural crops.

Horticulturists can work in industry, government or educational institutions or private collections. They can be cropping systems engineers, wholesale or retail business managers, propagators and tissue culture specialists (fruits, vegetables, ornamentals, and turf), crop inspectors, crop production advisers, extension specialists, plant breeders, research scientists, and of course, teachers.

Disciplines which complement horticulture include biology, botany, entomology, chemistry, mathematics, genetics, physiology, statistics, computer science, and communications, garden design, planting design. Plant science and horticulture courses include: plant materials, plant propagation, tissue culture, crop production, post-harvest handling, plant breeding, pollination management, crop nutrition, entomology, plant pathology, economics, and business. Some careers in horticultural science require a masters (MS) or doctoral (Ph.D) degree.

Horticulture is practiced in many gardens, "plant growth centres" and nurseries. Activities in nurseries range from preparing seeds and cuttings to growing fully mature plants. These are often sold or transferred to ornamental gardens or market gardens.

Horticulture has a very long history. The study and science of horticulture dates all the way back to the times of Alexander the Great, and has been going on ever since, with present day horticulturists such as Freeman S. Howlett, the revolutionary horticulturist. The origins of horticulture lie in the transition of human communities from nomadic hunter-gatherers to sedentary or semi-sedentary horticultural communities, cultivating a variety of crops on a small scale around their dwellings or in specialized plots visited occasionally during migrations from one area to the next. (such as the 'milpa' or maize field of Mesoamerican cultures). In forest areas such horticulture is often carried out in swiddens ('slash and burn' areas). A characteristic of horticultural communities is that useful trees are often to be found planted around communities or specially retained from the natural ecosystem.

Horticulture primarily differs from agriculture in two ways, firstly it generally encompasses a smaller scale of cultivation, using small plots of mixed crops rather than large fields of single crops. Secondly horticultural cultivations generally include a wide variety of crops, even including fruit trees with ground crops. Agricultural cultivations however as a rule focus on one primary crop. In pre-contact North America the semi-sedentary horticultural communities of the Eastern Woodlands (growing maize, squash and sunflower) contrasted markedly with the mobile hunter-gatherer communities of the Plains people. In Central America, Maya horticulture involved augmentation of the forest with useful trees such as papaya, avocado, cacao, ceiba and sapodilla. In the cornfields, multiple crops were grown such as beans (using cornstalks as supports), squash, pumpkins and chilli peppers, in some cultures tended mainly or exclusively by women.

Urban Forest

An *urban forest* is a forest or a collection of trees that grow within a city, town or a suburb. In a wider sense it may include any kind of woody plant vegetation growing in and around human settlements. In a narrower sense (also called *forest park*) it describes areas whose ecosystems are inherited from wilderness leftovers or remnants. Care and management of urban forests is called urban forestry.

Urban forests play an important role in ecology of human habitats in many ways: they filter air, water, sunlight, provide shelter to animals and recreational area for people. They moderate local climate, slowing wind and stormwater, and shading homes and businesses to conserve energy. They are critical in cooling the urban heat island effect, thus potentially reducing the number of unhealthful ozone days that plague major cities in peak summer months.

In many countries there is a growing understanding of the importance of the natural ecology in urban forests. There are numerous projects underway aimed at restoration and preservation of ecosystems, ranging from simple elimination of leaf-raking and elimination of invasive plants to full-blown reintroduction of original species and riparian ecosystems.

The benefits of urban trees are many, including beautification, reduction of the urban heat island effect, reduction of stormwater runoff, reduction of air pollution, reduction of energy costs through increased shade over buildings, enhancement of property values, improved wildlife habitat, and mitigation of overall urban environmental impact.

Social, Psychological, Recreational, Wildlife

The presence of trees reduces stress, and trees have long been seen to benefit the health of urban dwellers. The shade of trees and other urban green spaces make place for people to meet and socialize and play. The Biophilia hypothesis argues that people are instinctively drawn to nature, while Attention Restoration Theory goes on to demonstrate tangible improvements in medical, academic and other outcomes, from access to nature. Proper planning and community involvement are important for the positive results to be realized.

Trees provide nesting sites and food for birds and other animals. People appreciate watching, feeding, photographing, painting urban trees, and wildlife. Urban trees and wildlife help people maintain their connection with nature.

Economic Benefits

The economic benefits of trees have been understood for a long time. Recently, more of these benefits are becoming quantified. Quantification of the economic benefits of trees helps justify public and private expenditures to maintain them. One of the most obvious examples of economic utility is the deciduous tree planted on the south and west of a building. The shade shelters and cools the building during the summer, but allows the sun to warm it in the winter after the leaves fall. The USDA 'Guide' notes on page 17 that "Businesses flourish, people linger and shop longer, apartments and office space rent quicker, tenants stay longer, property values increase, new business and industry is attracted" by trees. The physical effects of trees — the shade (solar regulation), humidity control, wind control, erosion control, evaporative cooling, sound and visual screening, traffic control, pollution absorption and precipitation — all have economic benefits.

Air Pollution Reduction

As cities struggle to comply with air quality standards, the ways that trees can help to clean the air should not be overlooked. The most serious pollutants in the urban atmosphere are ozone, nitrogen oxides (NOx), sulfuric oxides (SOx) and particulate pollution. Ground-level ozone, or smog, is created by chemical reactions between NOx and volatile organic compounds (VOCs) in the presence of sunlight. High temperatures increase the rate of this reaction. Vehicle emissions, emissions from industrial facilities, gasoline vapours, and chemical solvents are the major sources of NOx and VOCs. Particulate pollution, or particulate matter (PM10 and PM25), is made up of microscopic solids or liquid droplets that can be inhaled and retained in lung tissue causing serious health problems. Most particulate pollution begins as smoke or diesel soot and can cause serious health risk to people with heart and lung diseases and irritation to healthy citizens. Trees are an important, cost-effective solution to reducing pollution and improving air quality.

Trees Reduce Temperatures and Smog

With an extensive and healthy urban forest air quality can be drastically improved. Trees help to lower air temperatures and the urban heat island affect in urban areas. This reduction of temperature not only lowers energy use, it also improves air quality, as the formation of ozone is dependent on temperature.

- As temperatures climb, the formation of ozone increases.

- Healthy urban forests decrease temperatures, and reduce the formation of ozone.
- Large shade trees can reduce local ambient temperatures by 3 to 5ºC.
- Maximum mid-day temperature reductions due to trees range from 0.04ºC to 0.2ºC per 1 per cent canopy cover increase.
- In Sacramento County, California, it was estimated that doubling the canopy cover to five million trees would reduce summer temperatures by 3 degrees. This reduction in temperature would reduce peak ozone levels by as much as 7 per cent and smoggy days by 50 per cent.

Lower Temperatures Reduce Emissions in Parking Lots

Temperature reduction from shade trees in parking lots lowers the amount of evaporative emissions from parked cars. Unshaded parking lots can be viewed as miniature heat islands, where temperatures can be even higher than surrounding areas. Tree canopies will reduce air temperatures significantly. Although the bulk of hydrocarbon emissions come from tailpipe exhaust, 16 per cent of hydrocarbon emissions are from evaporative emissions that occur when the fuel delivery systems of parked vehicles are heated. These evaporative emissions and the exhaust emissions of the first few minutes of engine operation are sensitive to local microclimate. If cars are shaded in parking lots, evaporative emissions from fuel and volatilized plastics will be greatly reduced.

- Cars parked in parking lots with 50 per cent canopy cover emit 8 per cent less through evaporative emissions than cars parked in parking lots with only 8 per cent canopy cover.
- Due to the positive effects trees have on reducing temperatures and evaporative emissions in parking

lots, cities like Davis, California, have established parking lot ordinances that mandate 50 per cent canopy cover over paved areas.

'Cold Start' Emissions

The volatile components of asphalt pavement evaporate more slowly in shaded parking lots and streets. The shade not only reduces emissions, but reduces shrinking and cracking so that maintenance intervals can be lengthened. Less maintenance means less hot asphalt (fumes) and less heavy equipment (exhaust). The same principle applies to asphalt-based roofing.

Active Pollutant Removal

Trees also reduce pollution by actively removing it from the atmosphere. Leaf stomata, the pores on the leaf surface, take in polluting gases which are then absorbed by water inside the leaf. Some species of trees are more susceptible to the uptake of pollution, which can negatively affect plant growth. Ideally, trees should be selected that take in higher quantities of polluting gases and are resistant to the negative affects they can cause.

A study across the Chicago region determined that trees removed approximately 17 tonnes of carbon monoxide (CO), 93 tonnes of sulfur dioxide (SO_2), 98 tonnes of nitrogen dioxide (NO_2), and 210 tonnes of ozone (O_3) in 1991.

Carbon Sequestration

Urban forest managers are sometimes interested in the amount of carbon removed from the air and stored in their forest as wood in relation to the amount of carbon dioxide released into the atmosphere while running tree maintenance equipment powered by fossil fuels.

Interception of Particulate Matter

In addition to the uptake of harmful gases, trees also act as filters intercepting airborne particles and reducing the amount of harmful particulate matter. The particles are captured by the surface area of the tree and its foliage. These particles temporarily rest on the surface of the tree, as they can be washed off by rainwater, blown off by high winds, or fall to the ground with a dropped leaf. Although trees are only a temporary host to particulate matter, if they did not exist, the temporarily-housed particulate matter would remain airborne and harmful to humans. Increased tree cover will increase the amount of particulate matter intercepted from the air.

- Large evergreen trees with dense foliage collect the most particulate matter.
- The Chicago study determined that trees removed approximately 234 tonnes of particulate matter less than 10 micrometres (PM10) in 1991.
- Large healthy trees greater than 75 cm in trunk diameter remove approximately 70 times more air pollution annually (1.4 kg/yr) than small healthy trees less than 10 cm in diameter (0.02 kg/yr).

Biogenic Volatile Organic Compounds

One important thing to consider when assessing the urban forest's effect on air quality is that trees emit some biogenic volatile organic compounds (BVOCs). These are the chemicals (primarily isoprene and monoterpenes) that make up the essential oils, resins, and other organic compounds that plants use to attract pollinators and repel predators. As mentioned above, VOCs react with nitrogen oxides (NOx) to form ozone. BVOCs account for less than 10 per cent of the total amount of VOCs and BVOCs emitted in urban areas. This means that BVOC emissions from trees can contribute to the formation of ozone. Although their contribution may be small compared with other sources, BVOC emissions could exacerbate a smog problem.

Trees that are well adapted to and thrive in certain environments should not be replaced just because they may be high BVOC emitters. The amount of emissions spent on maintaining a tree that may emit low amounts of BVOCs, but is not well suited to an area, could be considerable and outweigh any possible benefits of low BVOC emission rates.

Trees should not be labelled as polluters because their total benefits on air quality and emissions reduction far outweigh the possible consequences of BVOC emissions on ozone concentrations. Emission of BVOCs increase exponentially with temperature. Therefore, higher emissions will occur at higher temperatures. In desert climates, locally native trees adapted to drought conditions emit significantly less BVOCs than plants native to wet regions. As discussed above, the formation of ozone is also temperature dependent. Thus, the best way to slow the production of ozone and emission of BVOCs is to reduce urban temperatures and the effect of the urban heat island. As suggested earlier, the most effective way to lower temperatures is with an increased canopy cover.

These effects of the urban forest on ozone production have only recently been discovered by the scientific community, so extensive and conclusive research has not yet been conducted. There have been some studies quantifying the effect of BVOC emissions on the formation of ozone, but none have conclusively measured the effect of the urban forest. Important questions remain unanswered. For instance, it is unknown if there are enough chemical reactions between BVOC emissions and NOx to produce harmful amounts of ozone in urban environments. It is therefore, important for cities to be aware that this research is still continuing and conclusions should not be drawn before proper evidence has been collected. New research may resolve these issues.

Urban Forestry

Urban forestry is the careful care and management of urban forests, i.e., tree populations in urban settings for the purpose of improving the urban environment. Urban forestry advocates the role of trees as a critical part of the urban infrastructure. Urban foresters plant and maintain trees, support appropriate tree and forest preservation, conduct research and promote the many benefits trees provide. Urban forestry is practiced by municipal and commercial arborists, municipal and utility foresters, environmental policymakers, city planners, consultants, educators, researchers and community activists.

Management Goals and Objectives

Management goals should be based on an understanding of public attitudes, perceptions, and knowledge, a review of the agents in change, and the expressed needs and concerns of the community. These goals should be compared to a dynamic or temporal description of the resource based from inventory and management objectives.

Functions and Values

Function, the dynamic operation of the forest, includes biochemical cycles, gas exchange, primary productivity, competition, succession, and regeneration. In urban environments, forest functions are frequently related to the human environment. Trees are usually selected, planted, trimmed, and nurtured by people, often with specific intentions, as when a tree is planted in a front yard to shade the driveway and frame the residence. The functional benefits provided by this tree depend on structural attributes, such as species and location, as well as management activities that influence its growth, crown dimensions, and health. Urban forest functions are thus often oriented toward human outcomes, such as shade, beauty, and privacy. People develop emotional attachments to trees that give them special status and value. Removing hazardous trees can be difficult when it means severing the connection between residents and the trees they love. For many, feelings of attachment to trees in cities influences feelings for preservation of trees in forests.

Urban forests improve air quality, absorb rainwater, improve biodiversity and potentially allow recycling to 20 per cent of waste which is wood-based.

The social and even medical benefits of nature are also dramatic. Urban poverty is common to areas lacking green spaces. Visiting green areas in cities can counteract the stress of city life, renew vital energ. Simply being able to see a natural view out of the window improves self discipline in inner city girls.

Having regular access to woodland is desirable for schools, and indeed Forest kindergartens take children to visit substantial forests every day, whatever the weather. When such children go to primary school, teachers observe a significant improvement in reading, writing, mathematics, social skills and many other areas.

Challenges of Urban Forestry

Urban forestry is a practical discipline, which includes tree planting, care, and protection, and the overall management of trees as a collective resource. The urban environment presents the arboricultural challenges of limited root and canopy space, poor soil quality, deficiency or excess of water and light, heat, pollution, mechanical and chemical damage to trees, and mitigation of tree-related hazards. Management challenges include maintaining a tree and planting site inventory, quantifying and maximizing the benefits of trees, minimizing costs, obtaining and maintaining public support and funding, and establishing laws and policies for trees on public and on private land. Urban forestry presents many social issues that require addressing to allow urban forestry to be seen by the many as an advantage rather than a curse on their environment. Social issues include under funding and lack of management.

Urban Forestry in the United States

History: Tree warden laws in the New England states are important examples of some of the earliest and most far-sighted state urban forestry and forest conservation legislation. In 1896, the Massachusetts legislature passed the first tree warden law, and the other five New England states soon followed suit: Connecticut, Rhode Island, and New Hampshire in 1901, Vermont in 1904, and Maine in 1919. As villages and towns grew in population and wealth, ornamentation of public, or common, spaces with shade trees also increased. However, the ornamentation of public areas did not evolve into a social movement until the late 18th century, when private individuals seriously promoted and sponsored public beautification with shade and ornamental trees. Almost a century later, around 1850, institutions and organization were founded to promote ornamentation through private means.

In the 1890's, New England's 'Nail' laws enabled towns to take definitive steps to distinguish which shade trees were public. Chapter 196 of the 1890 Massachusetts Acts and Resolves stated that a public shade tree was to be designated by driving a nail or spike, with the letter M plainly impressed on its head, into the relevant trunk. Connecticut passed a similar law in 1893, except its certified nails and spikes bore the letter C.

In the United States, federal urban forestry policy is overseen by the USDA Forest Service, part of the Department of Agriculture. Much of the work on the ground is performed by non-profits funded by private donations and government grants.

Policy on urban forestry is less contentious and partisan than many other forestry issues, such as resource extraction in national forests.

Urban Forestry in Toronto

Toronto is a diverse city with a mosaic urban forest — a patchwork of unique situations made up of trees growing in the many residential yards, lining the public streets, and beautify public parks. Unlike the trees that grow in a wild setting, urban trees are faced with harsh conditions that can be a detriment to their health and growing potential. Soil compaction, air pollution, habitat fragmentation and competition from invasive species are some of the hardships city trees endure. Some neighbourhoods have a geriatric tree population; many mature trees that will reach the end of their lifespan very soon, with few young trees to replace them.

Some neighbourhoods suffer a serious lack of species diversity, with mainly ornamental, non-native or invasive tree species such as Bradford pear, Japanese tree lilac and Norway maple. Still other neighbourhoods, most often newly constructed subdivisions, lack tree cover completely.

Simply planting more trees cannot solve the problems faced by the urban forest. Through creative and innovative approaches the public, partnered with private enterprises can maximize the potential benefits of trees planted, and minimize the stresses they will have to overcome.

Although most people express a concern for urban trees and consider them very important, many lack the basic knowledge and skills needed to address and prevent the issues listed above. Collective action, or inaction, will make or break the future of the urban forest. Through fostering a sense of ownership amongst Toronto residents for this commonly owned resource, residents will enjoy better air quality and reduce their demand for energy.

Constraints to Urban Forestry

Resolving limitations will require coordinated efforts among cities, regions, and countries.

Loss of green space available growing space is limited in city centres. This problem is compounded by pressure to convert green space, parks, etc. into building sites.

Harsh growing conditions that makes tree survival an achievement. Lack of information on the tolerances of urban tree cultivars to environmental constraints. Poor tree selection which leads to problems in the future poor nursery stock and failure of post-care. Limited genetic diversity too have working tree inventories and very few communities have urban forest management plans. Lack of public awareness about the benefits of healthy urban forests and poor tree care practices by citizens and untrained arborists.

Tree

A *tree* is a perennial woody plant. It is most often defined as a woody plant that has many secondary branches supported clear of the ground on a single main stem or trunk with clear apical dominance. A minimum height specification at maturity is cited by some authors, varying from 3 m to 6 m; some authors set a minimum of 10 cm trunk diameter (30 cm girth). Woody plants that do not meet these definitions by having multiple stems and/or small size, are called shrubs. Compared with most other plants, trees are long-lived, some reaching several thousand years old and growing up to 115 m (379 ft) high.

Trees are an important component of the natural landscape because of their prevention of erosion and the provision of a weather-sheltered ecosystem in and under their foliage. They also play an important role in producing oxygen and reducing carbon dioxide in the atmosphere, as well as moderating ground temperatures. They are also elements in landscaping and agriculture, both for their aesthetic appeal and their orchard crops (such as apples). Wood from trees is a building material, as well as a primary energy source in many developing countries. Trees also play a role in many of the world's mythologies.

A tree is a plant form that occurs in many different orders and families of plants. Trees show a variety of growth forms, leaf type and shape, bark characteristics, and reproductive organs.

The tree form has evolved separately in unrelated classes of plants, in response to similar environmental challenges, making it a classic example of parallel evolution. With an estimate of 100,000 tree species, the number of tree species worldwide might total 25 per cent of all living plant species. The majority of tree species grow in tropical regions of the world and many of these areas have not been surveyed yet by botanists, making species diversity and ranges poorly understood.

The earliest trees were tree ferns, horsetails and lycophytes, which grew in forests in the Carboniferous Period; tree ferns still survive, but the only surviving horsetails and lycophytes are not of tree form. Later, in the Triassic Period, conifers, ginkgos, cycads and other gymnosperms appeared, and subsequently flowering plants in the Cretaceous Period. Most species of trees today are flowering plants (Angiosperms) and conifers. For the listing of examples of well-known trees and how they are classified, see List of tree genera.

A small group of trees growing together is called a *grove* or *copse*, and a landscape covered by a dense growth of trees is called a *forest*. Several biotopes are defined largely by the trees that inhabit them; examples are rainforest and taiga. A landscape of trees scattered or spaced across grassland (usually grazed or burned over periodically) is called a *savanna*. A forest of great age is called *old growth forest* or *ancient woodland* (in the UK). A young tree is called a sapling.

The parts of a tree are the roots, trunk(s), branches, twigs and leaves. Tree stems consist mainly of support and transport tissues (xylem and phloem). Wood consists of *xylem* cells, and bark is made of *phloem* and other tissues external to the vascular cambium. Trees may be grouped into *exogenous* and *endogenous* trees according to the way in which their stem diameter increases. Exogenous trees, which comprise the great majority of trees (all conifers, and almost all broadleaf trees), grow by the addition of new wood outwards, immediately under the bark. Endogenous trees, mainly in the monocotyledons (e.g., palms and dragon trees), but also cacti, grow by addition of new material inwards.

As an exogenous tree grows, it creates growth rings as new wood is laid down concentrically over the old wood. In species growing in areas with seasonal climate changes, wood growth produced at different times of the year may be visible as alternating light and dark, or soft and hard, rings of wood. In temperate climates, and tropical climates with a single wet-dry season alternation, the growth rings are annual, each pair of light and dark rings being one year of growth; these are known as annual rings. In areas with two wet and dry seasons each year, there may be two pairs of light and dark rings each year; and in some (mainly semi-desert regions with irregular rainfall), there may be a new growth ring with each rainfall. In tropical rainforest regions, with constant year-round climate, growth is continuous and the growth rings are not visible nor is there a change in the wood texture. In species with annual rings, these rings can be counted to determine the age of the tree, and used to date cores or even wood taken from trees in the past, a practice is known as the science of dendrochronology. Very few tropical trees can be accurately aged in this manner. Age determination is also impossible in endogenous trees.

The roots of a tree are generally embedded in earth, providing anchorage for the above-ground biomass and absorbing water and nutrients from the soil. It should be noted, however, that while ground nutrients are essential to a tree's growth the majority of its biomass comes from carbon dioxide absorbed from the atmosphere. Above ground, the trunk gives height to the leaf-bearing branches, aiding in competition with other plant species for sunlight. In many trees, the arrangement of the branches optimizes exposure of the leaves to sunlight.

Not all trees have all the plant organs or parts mentioned above. For example, most palm trees are not branched, the saguaro cactus of North America has no functional leaves, tree ferns do not produce bark, etc. Based on their general shape and size, all of these are nonetheless generally regarded as trees. A plant form that is similar to a tree, but generally having smaller, multiple trunks and/ or branches that arise near the ground, is called a shrub. However, no precise differentiation between shrubs and trees is possible. Given their small size, bonsai plants would not technically be 'trees', but one should not confuse reference to the form of a species with the size or shape of individual specimens. A spruce seedling does not fit the definition of a tree, but all spruces are trees.

Tallest Trees

The heights of the tallest trees in the world have been the subject of considerable dispute and much exaggeration. Modern verified measurements with laser rangefinders, other measuring devices, or with tape drop measurements made by tree climbers (such as those carried out by canopy researchers or members of groups like the U.S. Eastern Native Tree Society), have shown that some older measuring methods and measurements are often unreliable, sometimes producing exaggerations of 5 per cent to 15 per cent or more above the real height. Historical claims of trees growing to 130 m (427 ft), and even 150 m (492 ft), are now largely disregarded as unreliable, and attributed to human error. Historical records of fallen trees measured prostrate on the ground are considered to be somewhat more reliable. The following are now accepted as the top ten tallest reliably measured species:

- Coast Redwood (Sequoia sempervirens): 115.56 m (379.1 ft), Redwood National Park, California, United States.
- Australian Mountain-ash (Eucalyptus regnans): 99.6 m (326.8 ft), south of Hobart, Tasmania, Australia.
- Coast Douglas-fir (Pseudotsuga menziesii): 99.4 m (326.1 ft), Brummit Creek, Coos County, Oregon, United States.
- Sitka Spruce (Picea sitchensis): 96.7 m (317.3 ft), Prairie Creek Redwoods State Park, California, United States.
- Giant Sequoia (Sequoiadendron giganteum): 94.9 m (311.4 ft), Redwood Mountain Grove, Kings Canyon National Park, California, United States.
- Shorea faguetiana 88.3 m (289.7 ft) Tawau Hills National Park, in Sabah on the island of Borneo.
- Eucalyptus delegatensis 87.9 m (288.4 ft) Tasmania.
- Koompassia excelsa 85.8 m (281.5 ft).
- Shorea argentifolia 84.9 m (278.5 ft) Tawau Hills National Park, in Sabah.
- Shorea superba 84.4 m (276.9 ft) Tawau Hills National Park, in Sabah.

The girth of a tree is usually much easier to measure than the height, as it is a simple matter of stretching a tape round the trunk, and pulling it taut to find the circumference. Despite this, UK tree author Alan Mitchell made the following comment about measurements of yew trees:

> "The aberrations of past measurements of yews are beyond belief. For example, the tree at Tisbury has a well-defined, clean, if irregular bole at least 1.5 m long. It has been found to have a girth which has dilated and shrunk in the following way:

- 11.28 m (1834 Loudon), 9.3 m (1892 Lowe), 10.67 m (1903 Elwes and Henry), 9.0 m (1924 E. Swanton), 9.45 m (1959 Mitchell). . . . Earlier measurements have therefore been omitted".

  —Alan Mitchell; in a handbook "*Conifers in the British Isles*".

As a general standard, tree girth is taken at 'breast height'. This is cited as *dbh* (diameter at breast height) in tree and forestry literature. Breast height is defined differently in different situations, with most forestry measurements taking girth at 1.3 m above ground, while those who measure ornamental trees usually measure at 1.5 m above ground; in most cases this makes little difference to the measured girth. On sloping ground, the 'above ground' reference point is usually taken as the highest point on the ground touching the trunk, but some use the average between the highest and lowest points of ground . Some of the inflated old measurements may have been taken at ground level. Some past exaggerated measurements also result from measuring the complete next-to-bark measurement, pushing the tape in and out over every crevice and buttress.

Modern trends are to cite the tree's diameter rather than the circumference. Diameter of the tree is calculated by finding the medium diameter of the trunk, in most cases obtained by dividing the measured circumference by p; this assumes the trunk is mostly circular in cross-section (an oval or irregular cross-section would result in a mean diameter slightly greater than the assumed circle). Accurately measuring circumference or diameter is difficult in species with the large buttresses that are especially characteristic in many species of rainforest trees. Simple measurement of circumference of such trees can be misleading when the circumference includes much empty space between buttresses.

One further problem with measuring baobabs *Adansonia* is that these trees store large amounts of water in the very soft wood in their trunks. This leads to marked variation in their girth over the year though not more than about 2.5 per cent, swelling to a maximum at the end of the rainy season, minimum at the end of the dry season.

The stoutest living single-trunk species in diameter are:

- African Baobab *Adansonia digitata:* 15.9 m (52 ft), Glencoe Baobab (measured near the ground), Limpopo Province, South Africa. This tree split up in November 2009 and now the stoutest baobab could be Sunland Baobab (South Africa) with idealised diameter 10.64 m and correct circumference - 33.4 m.
- Montezuma Cypress *Taxodium mucronatum:* 11.62 m (38.1 ft), Árbol del Tule, Santa Maria del Tule, Oaxaca, Mexico. Note though that this diameter includes buttressing; the actual idealised diameter of the area of its wood is 9.38 m (30.8 ft).
- Giant Sequoia *Sequoiadendron giganteum:* 8.85 m (29 ft), General Grant tree, Grant Grove, California, United States.
- Coast Redwood *Sequoia sempervirens:* 7.9 m (25.9 ft), Lost Monarch Jedediah Smith Redwoods State Park, California, United States.
- Australian Oak *Eucalyptus obliqua:* 6.72 m (22 ft).
- Australian Mountain-ash *Eucalyptus regnans:* 6.52 m (21.4 ft).
- Western Redcedar *Thuja plicata:* 5.99 m (19.7 ft), Kalaloch Cedar, Olympic National Park.
- Sitka Spruce *Picea sitchensis:* 5.39 m (17.7 ft), Quinalt Lake Spruce, Olympic National Park.
- Alerce *Fitzroya cupressoides:* 5.0 m (16.4 ft).

An additional problem lies in instances where multiple trunks (whether from an individual tree or multiple trees) grow together. The Sacred Fig is a notable example of this, forming additional 'trunks' by growing adventitious roots down from the branches, which then thicken up when the root reaches the ground to form new trunks; a single Sacred Fig tree can have hundreds of such trunks.

The largest trees in total volume are those which are both tall and of large diameter, and in particular, which hold a large diameter high up the trunk. Measurement is very complex, particularly if branch volume is to be included as well as the trunk volume, so measurements have only been made for a small number of trees, and generally only for the trunk. No attempt has ever been made to include root volume. Measuring standards vary.

The top ten species measured so far are:

- Giant Sequoia *Sequoiadendron giganteum*: 1,487 m^3 (52,508 cu ft), General Sherman.
- Coast Redwood *Sequoia sempervirens*: 1,203 m^3 (42,500 cu ft), Lost Monarch.
- Montezuma Cypress *Taxodium mucronatum*: 750 m^3 (25,000 cu ft), Árbol del Tule.
- Western Redcedar *Thuja plicata*: 500 m^3 (17,650 cu ft), Quinault Lake Redcedar.
- Tasmanian Blue Gum *Eucalyptus globulus*: 368 m^3 (13,000 cu ft), Rullah Longatyle (Strong Girl, also Grieving Giant).
- Australian Mountain-ash *Eucalyptus regnans*: 360 m^3 (12,714 cu ft), Arve Big Tree.
- Coast Douglas-fir *Pseudotsuga menziesii* 349 m^3 (12,320 cu ft) Red Creek Tree.
- Sitka Spruce *Picea sitchensis* 337 m^3 (11,920 cu ft) Queets Spruce.

- Australian Oak *Eucalyptus obliqua*: 337 m^3 (11,920 cu ft) Gothmog.
- Alpine Ash *Eucalyptus delegatensis*: 286 m^3 (10,100 cu ft), located in Styx River Valley.

Smallest Trees

Many fully grown mature trees may be very short due to environmental factors or disease. However healthy and well grown specimens of a few species of tree only reach a height of a few centimetres. Amongst these Lepidothamnus laxifolius believed to be the shortest conifer in the world.

Oldest Trees

The oldest trees are determined by growth rings, which can be seen if the tree is cut down or in cores taken from the edge to the center of the tree. Accurate determination is only possible for trees which produce growth rings, generally those which occur in seasonal climates; trees in uniform non-seasonal tropical climates grow continuously and do not have distinct growth rings. It is also only possible for trees which are solid to the centre of the tree; many very old trees become hollow as the dead heartwood decays away. For some of these species, age estimates have been made on the basis of extrapolating current growth rates, but the results are usually little better than guesswork or wild speculation. White (1998) proposes a method of estimating the age of large and veteran trees in the United Kingdom through the correlation between a tree's stem diameter, growth character and age.

The verified oldest measured ages are:

- Great Basin Bristlecone Pine (Methuselah) *Pinus longaeva*: 4,844 years.
- Alerce *Fitzroya cupressoides*: 3,622 years.
- Giant Sequoia *Sequoiadendron giganteum*: 3,266 years.

- Sugi *Cryptomeria japonica*: 3,000 years.
- Huon-pine *Lagarostrobos franklinii*: 2,500 years.

Other species suspected of reaching exceptional age include European Yew *Taxus baccata* (probably over 2,000 years and Western Redcedar *Thuja plicata*.

The oldest reported age for an angiosperm tree is 2293 years for the Sri Maha Bodhi Sacred Fig (*Ficus religiosa*) planted in 288 BC at Anuradhapura, Sri Lanka; this is also the oldest human-planted tree with a known planting date.

Damage

El Grande, about 280 feet high, the most massive (though not the tallest) *Eucalyptus regnans* was accidentally killed by loggers burning-off the remains of legally loggable trees (less than 280 ft) that had been felled all around it.

The two major sources of tree damage are biotic (from living sources) and abiotic (from non-living sources). Biotic sources would include insects which might bore into the tree, deer which might rub bark off the trunk, or fungi, which might attach themselves to the tree.

Abiotic sources include lightning, vehicles impacts, and construction activities. Construction activities can involve a number of damage sources, including grade changes that prevent aeration to roots, spills involving toxic chemicals such as cement or petroleum products, or severing of branches or roots.

Both damage sources can result in trees becoming dangerous, and the term 'hazard trees' is commonly used by arborists, and industry groups such as power line operators. Hazard trees are trees which due to disease or other factors are more susceptible to falling during windstorms, or having parts of the tree fall.

The process of evaluating the danger a tree presents is based on a process called the quantified tree risk assessment.

Assessment as to labelling a tree a hazard tree can be based on a field examination. Assessment as a result of construction activities that will damage a tree is based on three factors; severity, extent and duration. Severity relates usually to the degree of intrusion into the TPZ and resultant root loss. Extent is frequently a percentage of a factor such as canopy, roots or bark, and duration is normally based on time. Root severing is considered permanent in time.

Trees are similar to people. Both can withstand massive amounts of some types of damage and survive, but even small amounts of certain types of trauma can result in death. Arborists are very aware that established trees will not tolerate any appreciable disturbance of the root system. However, lay people and construction professionals are seldom cognizant of how easily a tree can be killed.

One reason for confusion about tree damage from construction involves the dormancy of trees during winter. Another factor is that trees may not show symptoms of damage until 24-months or longer after damage has occurred. For that reason, persons uneducated in arboriculture science may not correlate the actual cause and resultant effect.

Various organizations, such as the International Society of Arboriculture, the British Standards Institute and the National Arborist Association (about 2007 renamed the Tree Industry Association), have long recognized the importance of construction activities that impact tree health. The impacts are important because they can result in monetary losses due to tree damage and resultant remediation or replacement costs, as well as violation of government ordinances or community or subdivision restrictions.

As a result, protocols for tree management prior to, during and after construction activities are well established, tested and refined. These basic steps are involved:

- Review of the construction plans
- Development of the related tree inventory
- Application of standard construction tree management protocols
- Assessment of potential for expected tree damages
- Development of a tree protection plan (providing for pre-, concurrent, and post construction damage prevention and remediation steps)
- Development of a tree protection plan
- Development of a remediation plan
- Implementation of tree protection zones (TPZ)
- Assessment of construction tree damage, post-construction.
- Implementation of the remediation plan.

International standards are uniform in analyzing damage potential and sizing TPZs (tree protection zones) to minimize damage. For mature to fully mature trees, the accepted TPZ comprises a 1.5-foot set-off for every 1-inch diameter of trunk. That means for a 10-inch tree, the TPZ would extend 15-feet in all directions from the base of the trunk at ground level.

For young/small trees with minimal crowns (and trunks less than 4-inches in diameter) a TPZ equal to 1-foot for every inch of trunk diameter may suffice. That means for a 3-inch tree, the TPZ would extend 3-feet in all directions from the base of the trunk at ground level. Detailed information on TPZs and related topics is available at minimal cost from organizations like the International Society for Arboriculture.

The tree has always been a cultural symbol. Common icons are the World tree, for instance Yggdrasil, and the tree of life. The tree is often used to represent nature or the environment itself. A common misconception is that trees get most of their mass from the ground. In fact, 99 per cent of a tree's mass comes from the air.

These most likely use diameter measured at breast height, 4.5 feet (140 cm) above ground — not the larger base diameter. A general model for any year and diameter is Value = 17.27939* (diameter ^2)*1.022^ (year -1985) assuming 2.2 per cent inflation per year. (Note, the right side of this equation is written to paste into Excel or Google to perform the calculation.) Extrapolations from any model can cause problems, so tree value estimates for diameters larger than 30 inches might have to be capped so trees do not not exceed 27 per cent of the total appraised property value.

Arborist

An *arborist*, *arboriculturalist* or *tree surgeon* is a professional in the practice of arboriculture, which is the management and maintenance of ornamental or shade trees. Work can include tree surgery and also care of shrubs, vines, and other perennial woody plants. An arborist is distinct from a forester, or from a logger. Those professions may have much in common, but the scope of work is different. Arborists frequently focus on health and safety of individual trees, or wooded landscapes, rather than managing forests or harvesting wood.

To work near power wires either additional training is required for arborists or they need to be Certified Line Clearance trimmers or Utility Arborists (there may be different terminology for various countries). There is a variety of minimum distances that must be kept from power wires depending on voltage, however the common distance for low voltage lines in urban settings is 10 feet (about 3 metres).

Arborists who climb (as not all do) can use a variety of techniques to ascend into the tree. The least invasive, and most popular technique used is to ascend on rope. When personal safety is an issue, or the tree is being removed, arborists may use 'hooks', (also known as 'gaffs' or 'spurs') attached to their boots with straps to ascend and work. Hooks wound the tree, leaving small holes where each step has been.

An arborist's work may involve very large and complex trees, or ecological communities and their abiotic components in the context of the landscape ecosystem. These may require monitoring and treatment to ensure they are healthy, safe, and suitable to property owners or community standards. This work may include some or all of the following: planting; transplanting; pruning; structural support; preventing, or diagnosing and treating phytopathology or parasitism; preventing or interrupting grazing or predation; installing lightning protection; and removing vegetation deemed as hazardous, an invasive species, a disease vector, or a weed.

Arborists may also plan, consult, write reports and give legal testimony. While some aspects of this work are done on the ground or in an office, much of it is done by arborists who climb the trees with ropes, harnesses and other equipment. Lifts and cranes may be used too. The work of all arborists is not the same. Some may just perform consulting; others may perform climbing, pruning and planting: a combination. Arborists gain certification and qualifications in a variety of ways depending on location such as country. It is important you know what type of arborist you need as for instance not all climb nor do all write reports and consult.

In Australia education and training is stream lined country wide and referred to as AQF. There are varying levels of qualification.

In USA a Certified Arborist (or 'CA') is a professional who has over three years experience and has passed a rigorous written test from the International Society of Arboriculture. Other designations include Municipal Specialist, Utility Specialist and Board Certified Master Arborist (BCMA).

Cultural Practices

Trees may need pruning for health and good structure, for aesthetic reasons, and to permit people to walk under them. They might also require other care to improve their chances for survival, including treatments in response to damage from biotic or abiotic factors. Trees in urban landscape settings are often subject to human and natural disturbances above and below ground, and in need of solutions provided by arborists. Timing or methods depend on the species of tree and the purpose of the work, and a thorough knowledge of local species and environments is necessary to determine the best practices. Trees may also require pruning to keep them away from wires, fences and buildings.

There can be a vast difference between the techniques and practices of professional arborists and those (without adequate training) who simply 'trim trees'. Some practices of (uneducated) tree workers are considered unacceptable by modern arboriculture standards. One example of an 'unacceptable' practice is called 'topping', 'lopping' or 'hatracking', when entire tops of trees or main stems are cut off, causing detrimental effects; generally done by cross-cutting the main stem or leaders, leaving big flat topped stubs.

Pruning should only be done with a specific purpose in mind. Every cut is a wound, and every leaf lost is removal of some photosynthetic potential. Proper pruning can be helpful in many ways, but should always be done with the minimum amount of live tissue removed.

In recent years, research has proven that wound dressings such as paint, tar or other coverings are unnecessary and may harm trees. The coverings may encourage growth of decay-causing fungi. Proper pruning, by cutting through branches at the right location, can do more to limit decay than wound dressing.

Chemicals can be applied to trees for insect or disease control through spraying, soil application, stem injections or spraying. Compacted or disturbed soils can be improved in various ways.

Arborists can also assess trees to determine the health, structure, safety or feasibility within a landscape and in proximity to humans. Modern arboriculture has progressed in technology and sophistication from practices of the past, and many current practices are based on knowledge gained through recent research, including the widely respected intensive work by the late Alex Shigo, considered as one 'fathers' of modern arboriculture.

Depending on the jurisdiction, there are a number of legal issues surrounding the practices of arborists and of urban tree management in general, including boundary issues, public safety issues, 'heritage' trees of community value; and 'neighbour' issues such as ownership, obstruction of views, impacts of roots crossing boundaries, nuisance problems, disease or insect quarantines, and safety of nearby trees.

Arborists are frequently consulted to establish the factual basis of disputes involving trees, or by private property owners seeking to avoid legal liability through the duty of care. Arborists may be asked to assess the value of a tree in the process of an insurance claim for trees damaged or destroyed, or to recover damages resulting from tree theft or vandalism. In cities with tree preservation orders an arborist's evaluation of tree hazard may be required before a property owner may remove a tree, or to assure the protection of trees in development plans and during construction operations. Homeowners who have entered into contracts with a homeowner's association may need an arborist's professional opinion of a hazardous condition prior to removing a tree, or may be obligated to assure the protection of the views of neighbouring properties prior to planting a tree or in the course of pruning. Arborists may be consulted in forensic investigations where the evidence of a crime can be determined within the growth rings of a tree, for example. Arborists may be engaged by one member of a dispute in order to identify factual information about trees useful to that member of the dispute, or they can be engaged as an expert witness providing unbiased scientific knowledge in a court case. Homeowners associations seeking to write restrictive covenants, or legislative bodies seeking to write laws involving trees, may seek the counsel of arborists in order to avoid future difficulties.

Arborist Training, Reference Materials and Continuing Education

The study materials considered to be the reference canon for arborists seeking to advance from entry level to mastery of the trade in arboricultural services are the following:

- *Arboriculture:* Integrated Management of Landscape Trees, Brooms, Shrubs, and Vines, 4th edition (Harris et al.) — the standard text for introductory arboriculture, and the primary reference for working arborists.
- ANSI A300 standards for tree care operations (TCIA, all parts) — industry standards.
- ANSI Z133.1 standard for tree care operations (ISA) — industry standards.
- ANSI Z60 standard for nursery stock (ANLA) — industry standards.
- Best Management Practices (ISA, all topics).
- Plant Health Care for Woody Ornamentals (Lloyd et al.)
- Abiotic Disorders of Landscape Plants — A Diagnostic Guide (Costello et al.)
- *Trees and Development:* A Technical Guide to Preservation of Trees During Land Development (Matheny and Clark).

- Manual of Woody Landscape Plants (Dirr)
- An Illustrated Guide to Pruning, 2nd edition (Gilman)
- Principles and Practice of Planting Trees and Shrubs (Watson and Himelick).
- Arborists' Certification Study Guide (Lilly)
- Plant Physiology (Kozlowski).
- Urban Soils: Applications and Practices (Craul).
- A New Tree Biology (Shigo) — the classic text by the man widely considered the father of modern arboriculture, Alex Shigo.
- The Landscape Below Ground; Parts I and II (Neely and Watson).
- Arboriculture and the Law (Merullo).
- Trees and Building Sites Conference Proceedings (Watson and Neely).
- The Art and Science of Practical Rigging (Donzelli et al.).
- A Photographic Guide to the Evaluation of Hazard Trees in Urban Areas (Matheny and Clark).
- Diseases of Trees and Shrubs (Sinclair et al.)
- Evaluating Tree Defects (Hayes).
- Guide for Plant Appraisal, 9th edition (CTLA).
- Insects that feed on trees and shrubs (Johnson et al.)
- Tree structure and mechanics conference proceedings: How Trees Stand Up and Fall Down (Smiley et al.)
- Journal of Arboriculture — (academic research periodical.)
- Pesticide information.
- Urban Forestry: Planning and Managing Urban Greenspaces (Robert Miller).
- Natural Disaster Damage to vegetation.

Other significant study materials and references for arborists include:

- USDA soil surveys
- Soil science (Hausenbuiller)
- Urban soil in landscape design (Craul)
- Built environment (Bartuska)
- Design with nature
- Principles and applications of soil microbiology (Sylvia et al.)
- The biology of symbiotic fungi (Cooke)
- Mycology — plant pathology internet guide book (Kraska)
- Forest Entomology: Ecology and Management (Coulson & Witter)
- Plants of the Pacific Northwest (Pojar), or similar local reference.
- Trees of Seattle (Jacobson), or similar local reference.
- Natural Vegetation of Oregon and Washington (Franklin), or similar local reference.
- The Use and Significance of Pesticides in the Environment (McEwen).
- The body language of trees (Mattheck).
- Trees (Coombes).
- *Wild neighbours:* The humane approach to living with wildlife.
- IPM world textbook (Radcliff, online).

Arborist Organisations

- The tree care industry association, formerly the National Arborist Association, is a public and professional non-profit organization for the arboriculture field. It has more than 2,000 member companies representing over a dozen countries. TCIA's Accreditation programme certifies that tree care companies that have been inspected and accredited based on adherence to industry standards for performance and safety; maintenance of trained, professional staff; and dedication to ethics and quality in business practices. In addition, they provide safety and educational programmes, guidelines for tree service operations, ANSI A300 tree pruning standards, and consumer resources.

- The international society of arboriculture, a non-profit organization, maintains a list of ISA Certified Arborists who have passed a written exam and demonstrated a basic level of knowledge in arboriculture. There are also additional classifications of certified arborists with Certified Arborist/Utility Specialist for those who work near power lines, and Certified Arborist/Municipal Specialist for those who deal mostly with community trees. Other certifications exist for Certified Tree Workers, and the highest level of certification, the Board Certified Master Arborist.
- The American society of consulting arborists is an organization whose membership is exclusive to those with either a certain level of industry experience, plus higher educational experience or continuing education; some members may achieve a higher status by fulfilling the requirements to become a Registered Consulting Arborist. Consulting arborists generally specialize in the areas of ethics, law, land planning and development, and tree valuation, among others. Consulting arborists are often called on for legal testimony and report writing in various instances where a particular authority on trees is necessary for consequent actions.
- In the UK, the principal organisation representing arborists is the Arboricultural Association. The

association maintain a register of consultants who have demonstrated a high level of technical arboricultural knowledge, and operate an Approved Contractor scheme. This scheme assesses both the technical competence and business practices of arboricultural contractors. Searching for approved contractors is possible through the tree-care.info 'Find an Arborist' area and the 'UK Arborist Directory'.

- The European Arboriculture Council is a European group of arboriculture organizations from various countries.
- Plant Amnesty is a public education and advocacy group, based in Seattle, dedicated to promoting proper pruning methods. Founded in 1987, Plant Amnesty became an international resource for arborists and their clients in the mid 1990's.

Tree Planting

Tree planting is the process of transplanting tree seedlings, generally for forestry, land reclamation, or landscaping purposes. It differs from the transplantation of larger trees in arboriculture, and the lower cost but slower and less reliable distribution of tree seeds.

It is a silviculture activity known as reforestation. It involves planting seedlings over an area of land where the forest has been harvested or damaged by fire or disease or insects. Tree planting is carried out in many different parts of the world, and strategies may differ widely across nations, regions and individual reforestation companies. Tree planting is grounded in forest science, and if performed properly can result in the successful regeneration of a deforested area. Reforestation is the commercial logging industry's answer to the large-scale destruction of old growth forests, but a planted forest rarely replicates the biodiversity and complexity of a natural forest.

Because trees remove carbon dioxide from the air as they grow, tree planting can be used as a geoengineering technique to remove CO_2 from the atmosphere.

TREE PLANTING BY COUNTRY

Canada

Most tree planting in Canada is carried out by private reforestation companies. Reforestation companies compete with one another for contracts from logging companies, whose annual allowable cut for the following year is based upon how much money they invest into reforestation and other silvicultural practices. Tree planting is typically piece work and tree prices can vary widely depending on the difficulty of the terrain and on the winning contract's bid price. As a result, there is a saying among planters: "There is no bad land, only bad contracts."

Tree planting is seasonal labour and has become a popular form of employment for young Canadian adults, many of whom spend their summers planting trees in order to pay their university tuitions. In British Columbia, where the season is longer, tree planting is considered to be more of a career or profession than short-term summer employment. Although tree planting is both psychologically and physically challenging, hard workers can typically earn well above the average student income. However, the learning curve is quite steep, so many planters do not reap the attractive economic benefits their first season. This, combined with the need for the potential treeplanter to buy all of the equipment needed for the job (several hundreds of dollars worth), makes becoming a treeplanter a multi year investment for most.

Tree planting crews often do not permanently reside in the areas where they work, thus much planting is based out of motels or bush camps. Bush camp accommodations usually consist of a mess tent, cook shack, dry goods tent, first aid tent, freshly dug outhouses, and a shower tent or trailer. Planters are responsible for bringing either a tent or car to sleep in. A camp also contains camp cooks and support staff.

Planting is carried out in accordance to the client's specifications, and planters are expected to learn the quality standards for each contract that they work on. Planted clearcuts are spot checked on a regular basis. Although quality concerns vary across contracts, spot checkers are typically looking for such things as: species appropriate site choice, species appropriate spacing, how tight the seedlings are in the ground, how straight the seedlings are, and whether or not the seedlings have been damaged. These concerns vary from region to region, and from contract to contract.

The average BC planter plants 1 600 trees per day, but it is not uncommon for veterans to plant 2000-3000 trees per day while working in the BC interior. These numbers are higher in central and eastern Canada, where the terrain is generally faster, however the price per tree is slightly lower as a result. Planters typically work 8-10 hours per day with an additional 1 to 2 hours of (usually) unpaid travelling time. Work weeks on British Columbian planting contracts are usually 4-5 days long, with 1-2 days off. In Ontario, work weeks are generally 5-6 days long, with 1 day off.

Quite often, tree planting contractors will deduct some of the cost associated with the operation of the contract directly from the treeplanter's daily earned wages. These imposed fees typically vary from \$10 to \$30 per day, and are referred to as 'camp costs'. In *some* cases, rookie treeplanters end up owing their employer money for the first few pay periods.

Once inflation is factored in, real treeplanter earnings have declined for many years in Canada. This has adversely affected the sector's ability to attract and retain workers . Higher wages and much better working conditions in many other industries, from construction, to oil and gas, and even information technology, has led to fewer Canadian young people wanting to plant trees.

Based on statistics for British Columbia, the average treeplanter: lifts a cumulative weight of over 1 000 kilograms, bends more than 200 times per hour, drives the shovel into the ground more than 200 times per hour and travels over 16 kilometers with a heavy load, every day of the entire season.

The reforestation industry has an average annual injury rate of approximately 22 claims per 100 workers, per year. It is often difficult and sometimes dangerous.

Great Britain

Planting in Britain is commonly referred to as *restocking*, when it takes place on land that has recently been harvested. When occurring on previously unforested land it is known as *new planting*. Under the British system, in order to acquire the necessary permissions to clear fell, the landowner must agree a management plan with the Forestry Commission (the regulatory body for all things forestry) which must include proposals for the re-establishment of tree cover on the land. Planting contractors will be engaged by the landowner/management company, a contract drawn up and work will typically take place from November to April when the transplants are dormant.

Planting is part of the rotational nature of much British plantation forestry. Productive tree crops are planted and subsequently clear felled. Some form of soil cultivation may take place and the ground is then restocked. Where the production of timber is a management priority, a prescribed stocking density must be achieved. For coniferous species this will be a minimum of 2500 stems per hectare at year 5 (from planting). Planting at this density has been shown to favour the development of straighter knot free logs.

Planters are normally paid under piece work terms and an experienced worker will plant around 1500 trees a day under most conditions.

New Zealand

Kaingaroa Forest in New Zealand is the largest planted forest in the southern hemisphere. It is one of the many plantation forests planted since European settlement. The Monterey Pine (*Pinus radiata*) is commonly used for plantations since a fast growing cultivar suitable for a wide range of conditions has been developed.

Government agencies, environmental organisations and private trusts carry out tree planting for conservation and climate change mitigation. While some work is carried out by private enterprise there are also planting days organised for volunteers. Landcare Research use planted forests for their EBEX21 system for greenhouse gas emissions mitigations.

The development of markets for tradeable pollution permits in recent years have opened up a new source of funding for tree planting projects: carbon offsets. The creation of carbon offsets from tree planting projects hinges on the notion that trees help to mitigate climate change by sequestering carbon dioxide as they grow. However, the science linking trees and climate change is largely unsettled, and trees remain a controversial source of offsets.

Climate Impacts

Climate scientists believe that human-induced global deforestation is responsible for 18-25 per cent of global climate change. The United Nations, World Bank and other leading nongovernmental organizations are encouraging reforestation, avoided deforestation and other projects that encourage tree planting to mitigate the effects of climate change.

Trees sequester carbon through photosynthesis, converting carbon dioxide and water into molecular dioxygen (O_2) and plant organic matter, such as carbohydrates (e.g., cellulose). Hence, forests that grow in area or density and thus increase in organic biomass will reduce atmospheric CO_2 levels. (Carbon is released as CO_2 if a tree or its lumber burns or decays, but as long as the forest is able to grow back at the same rate as its biomass is lost due to oxidation of organic carbon, the net result is carbon neutral.) In their 2001 assessment, the IPCC estimated the potential of biological mitigation options (mainly tree planting) is on the order of 100 Gigatonnes of carbon (cumulative) by 2050, equivalent to about 10 per cent to 20 per cent of projected fossil fuel emissions during that period.

However, the global cooling effect of forests from carbon sequestration is not the only factor to be considered. For example, the planting of new forests may initially release some of the area's existing carbon stores into the atmosphere. Specifically, the conversion of peat bogs into oil palm plantations has made Indonesia the world's third largest producer of greenhouse gases.

Compared to less vegetated lands, forests affect climate in three main ways:

- Cooling the earth by functioning as carbon sinks.
- Cooling the earth by adding water vapour to the atmosphere and thereby increasing cloudiness.
- Warming the Earth by absorbing a high percentage of sunlight due to the low reflectivity of a forest's dark surfaces. This warming effect, or reduced albedo, is large where evergreen forests, which have very low reflectivity, shade snow cover, which is highly reflective.

To date, most tree-planting offset strategies have taken only the first effect into account. A study published in December 2005 combined all these effects and found that tropical forestation has a large net cooling effect, because of increased cloudiness and because of high tropical growth and carbon sequestration rates.

Trees grow three times faster in the tropics than in temperate zones; each tree in the rainy tropics removes about 22 kilograms (50 pounds) of carbon dioxide from the atmosphere each year. However, this study found little to no net global cooling from tree planting in temperate climates, where warming due to sunlight absorption by trees counteracts the global cooling effect of carbon sequestration. Furthermore, this study confirmed earlier findings that reforestation of colder regions — where long periods of snow cover, evergreen trees, and slow sequestration rates prevail — probably results in global warming. According to Ken Caldeira, a study co-author from the Carnegie Institution for Science, "To plant forests outside of the tropics to mitigate climate change is a waste of time."

His premise that grassland reflects more sun, keeping temperatures lower, is, however, applicable only in arid regions. A well-watered lawn, for example, is as green as a tree, but absorbs far less CO_2. Deciduous trees also have the advantage of providing shade in the summer and sunlight in the winter; so these trees, when planted close to houses, can be utilized to help increase energy efficiency of these houses.

This study remains controversial and criticized for assuming dark coloured trees might replace the frozen, white tundra in the upper northern hemisphere. Regular tree planting projects typically take place on lands that are only slightly different in colour. The warming impact was also measured over hundreds of years, rather than a 30-70 year time horizon most climate experts believe we have to fix climate change.

Furthermore, the described warming effect (of temperate and boreal latitude forest) is only apparent once the trees have grown to create a dense 'close canopy', and it is at precisely this point that trees grown for offset purposes should be harvested and their absorbed carbon fixed for the long-term as timber.

Costs

While the benefits of tree planting are subject to debate, the costs are low compared to many other mitigation options. The IPCC has concluded that "The mitigation costs through forestry can be quite modest (US$0.1-US$20/metric ton carbon dioxide) in some tropical developing countries. . . . The costs of biological mitigation, therefore, are low compared to those of many other alternative measures". The cost effectiveness of tropical reforestation is due not only to growth rate, but also to farmers from tropical developing countries who voluntarily plant and nurture tree species which can improve the productivity of their lands. As little as US$90 will plant 900 trees, enough to annually remove as much carbon dioxide as is annually generated by the fossil-fuel usage of an average United States.

Types of Trees Planted

The type of tree planted may have great influence on the environmental outcomes. Planting the wrong kind of trees, such as monocultures of eucalyptus where they are not native species, can devastate the lands of the local people. However, it is often much more profitable to outside interests to plant non-native fast-growing trees, such as eucalyptus or pine (e.g., *Pinus radiata* or *Pinus caribaea*), even though the environmental and biodiversity benefits of such monoculture plantations are not comparable to native forest, and such offset projects are frequently objects of controversy.

To promote the growth of native ecosystems, many environmentalists advocate only indigenous trees be planted. A practical solution is to plant tough, fast-growing native tree species which begin rebuilding the land. Planting non-invasive trees that assist in the natural return of indigenous species is called "assisted natural regeneration." There are many such species that can be planted, of which about 12 are in widespread use, such as *Leucaena leucocephala*.

Grafting

Grafting is a method of asexual plant propagation widely used in agriculture and horticulture where the tissues of one plant are encouraged to fuse with those of another. It is most commonly used for the propagation of trees and shrubs grown commercially.

In most cases, one plant is selected for its roots, and this is called the *stock* or *rootstock*. The other plant is selected for its stems, leaves, flowers, or fruits and is called the *scion*. The scion contains the desired genes to be duplicated in future production by the stock/scion plant.

In stem grafting, a common grafting method, a shoot of a selected, desired plant cultivar is grafted onto the stock of another type. In another common form called budding, a dormant side bud is grafted on the stem of another stock plant, and when it has fused successfully, it is encouraged to grow by cutting out the stem above the new bud.

For successful grafting to take place, the vascular cambium tissues of the stock and scion plants must be placed in contact with each other. Both tissues must be kept alive until the graft has taken, usually a period of a few weeks. Successful grafting only requires that a vascular connection takes place between the two tissues. A physical weak point often still occurs at the graft, because the structural tissue of the two distinct plants, such as wood, may not fuse.

- ***Dwarfing:*** To induce dwarfing or cold tolerance or other characteristics to the scion. Most apple trees in modern orchards are grafted on to dwarf or semi-dwarf trees planted at high density. They provide more fruit per unit of land, higher quality fruit, and reduce the danger of accidents by harvest crews working on ladders.
- ***Ease of propagation:*** Because the scion is difficult to propagate vegetatively by other means, such as by cuttings. In this case, cuttings of an easily rooted plant are used to provide a rootstock. In some cases, the scion may be easily propagated, but grafting may still be used because it is commercially the most cost-effective way of raising a particular type of plant.
- ***Hybrid breeding:*** To speed maturity of hybrids in fruit tree breeding programmes. Hybrid seedlings may take ten or more years to flower and fruit on their own roots. Grafting can reduce the time to flowering and shorten the breeding programme.
- ***Hardiness:*** Because the scion has weak roots or the roots of the stock plants have roots tolerant of difficult conditions. e.g. many showy Western Australian plants are sensitive to dieback on heavy soils, common in urban gardens, and are grafted onto hardier eastern Australian relatives. Grevilleas and eucalypts are examples.
- ***Sturdiness:*** In order to provide a strong, tall trunk for certain ornamental shrubs and trees. In these cases, a graft is made at a desired height on a stock plant with a strong stem. This is used to raise 'standard' roses, which are rose bushes on a high stem, and it is also used for some ornamental trees, such as certain weeping cherries.

- ***Pollen source:*** To provide pollenizers. For example, in tightly planted or badly planned apple orchards of a single variety, limbs of crab apple may be grafted at regularly spaced intervals onto trees down rows, say every fourth tree. This takes care of pollen needs at blossom time, yet does not confuse pickers who might otherwise mix varieties while harvesting, as the mature crab apples are so distinct from other apple varieties.
- ***Repair:*** To repair damage to the trunk of a tree which would prohibit nutrient flow, such as the stripping of the bark by rodents which completely girdles the trunk. In this case a bridge graft may be used to connect the tissues receiving flow from the roots to the tissues above the damage which have been severed from the flow. Where a watersprout, basal shoot or sapling of the same species is growing nearby, any of these can be grafted to the area above the damage by a method called inarch grafting. These alternatives to scions must be of the correct length to span the gap of the wound.
- ***Changing cultivars:*** To change the cultivar in a fruit orchard to a more profitable cultivar, called *topworking*. It may be faster to graft a new cultivar onto existing limbs of established trees than to replant an entire orchard.
- ***Maintain consistency:*** Apples are notorious for their genetic variability, even differing in multiple characteristics, such as, size, colour, and flavour, of fruits located on the same tree. In the commercial farming industry, consistency is maintained by grafting a scion with desired fruit traits onto a hardy stock.

Curiosities

A practice sometimes carried out by gardeners is to graft related potatoes and tomatoes so that both are produced on the same plant, one above ground and one underground.

Cacti of widely different forms are sometimes grafted on to each other.

Multiple cultivars of fruits such as apples are sometimes grafted on a single tree. This so-called 'family tree' provides more fruit variety for small spaces such as a suburban backyard, and also takes care of the need for pollenizers. The drawback is that the gardener must be sufficiently trained to prune them correctly, or one strong variety will usually 'take over'.

Ornamental and functional, tree shaping uses grafting techniques to join separate trees or parts of the same tree to itself. Furniture, hearts, entry archways are examples. Axel Erlandson was a prolific tree shaper who grew over 75 mature specimens.

Approach

Approach grafting or inarching is used to join together plants that are otherwise difficult to join. The plants are grown close together, and then joined so that each plant has roots below and growth above the point of union. Both scion and stock retain their respective parents that may or may not be removed after joining. Also used in pleaching. The graft can be successfully accomplished any time of year.

Budding

T Budding

Grafting with a single eye or bud. Normally performed at the height of the growing season by inserting a dormant bud into a shallow slice under the rind of the tree. The bud is sealed from drying and bound in place. There are many styles of budding depending on the cutting and fitting methods, the most popular being shield budding.

Other budding styles include the inverted T, patch budding, double shield, flute budding and chip budding.

Cleft

The most common form of grafting is cleft grafting. The stock is simply split and the scion is inserted. It is best if the stock is 2-7 cm (0.79-2.8′) in diameter and has 3-5 buds, and the cleft is around 3 cm (1.2′) deep. is cut in a wedge shape and inserted into the tree with the cambium. The bare stock is covered with grafting compound, otherwise the cambium layer quickly dries and the graft fails.

Whip

The whip graft is considered the most difficult to master, but has the highest rate of success. It is the most common graft used in top-dressing commercial fruit trees. It is limited to stock less than ½′ (1.3 cm) diameter, with the ideal diameter closer to 3/8′ (0.95 cm) . It offers the highest cambium overlap between the 2 species, increasing the rate of success. The elongated 'Z' shape adds strength, removing the need for a companion rod in the first season.

Stub

Stub grafting is a technique that requires less stock than cleft grafting, and retains the shape of a tree. Also scions are generally of 6-8 buds in this process.

An incision is made into the branch 1 cm (0.39′) long, then the scion is wedged and forced into the branch. The scion should be at an angle of at most 35° to the parent tree so that the crotch remains strong. The graft is covered with grafting compound.

After the graft has taken, the branch is removed and treated a few cm above the graft, to be fully removed when the graft is strong.

Awl

Awl grafting takes the least resources and the least time. It is best done by an experienced grafter, as it is possible to accidentally drive the tool too far into the stock, reducing the scion's chance of survival. Awl grafting can be done by using a screwdriver to make a slit in the bark, not penetrating the cambium layer completely. Then inset the wedged scion into the incision.

Veneer

Veneer grafting, or *inlay* grafting, is a method used for stocks larger than three centimeters in diameter. The scion is recommended to be about as thick as a pencil. Clefts are made of the same size as the scion on the side of the branch, not on top. The scion end is shaped as a wedge, inserted, and wrapped with tape to the scaffolding branches to give it more strength.

Natural Grafting

Tree branches and more often roots of the same species will sometimes naturally graft, this is called *inosculation*. When roots make physical contact with each other they often grow together. A group of trees can share water and mineral nutrients via root grafts, which may be advantageous to weaker trees, and may also form a larger rootmass as an adaptation to promote fire resistance and regeneration as exemplified by the California Black Oak.

A problem with root grafts is that they allow transmission of certain pathogens, such as Dutch elm disease. Inosculation also sometimes occurs where two stems on the same tree, shrub or vine make contact with each other. This is common in plants such as strawberries and potatoes.

Graft Hybrids

Occasionally, a so-called 'graft hybrid' can occur where the tissues of the stock continue to grow within the scion. Such a plant can produce flowers and foliage typical of both plants as well as shoots intermediate between the two. The best-known example is probably +*Laburnocytisus* 'Adamii', a graft hybrid between laburnum and broom, which originated in a nursery near Paris, France in 1825. This small tree bears yellow flowers typical of *Laburnum anagyroides*, purple flowers typical of *Chamaecytisus purpureus* and curious coppery-pink flowers which show characteristics of both 'parents'.

Scientific Uses

Grafting has been important in flowering research. Leaves or shoots from plants induced to flower can be grafted onto uninduced plants and transmit a floral stimulus that induces them to flower.

The transmission of plant viruses has been studied using grafting. Virus indexing involves grafting a symptomless plant that is suspected of carrying a virus onto an indicator plant that is very susceptible to the virus.

Herbaceous Grafting

Grafting is often done for non-woody and vegetable plants (tomato, cucumber, eggplant and watermelon). Tomato grafting is very popular in Asia and Europe, and is gaining popularity in the United States. The main advantage of grafting is for disease-resistant rootstocks. In Japan there is an automated process using grafting robots.

History

Grafting with detached scions has been practiced for thousands of years. It was in use by the Chinese before 2000 B.C and spread to the rest of Eurasia. The practice was almost commonplace in ancient Greece. Without the development of grafting, heterosexual fruit trees such as apples and cherries would never had been domesticated as their natural sexual reproductive method prevents useful genes from being passed on consistently.

7 Plant

Plants are living organisms belonging to the kingdom *Plantae*. They include familiar organisms such as trees, herbs, bushes, grasses, vines, ferns, mosses, and green algae. The scientific study of plants, known as botany, has identified about 3,50,000 extant species of plants, defined as seed plants, bryophytes, ferns and fern allies. As of 2004, some 2,87,655 species had been identified, of which 2,58,650 are flowering and 18,000 bryophytes. *Green plants*, sometimes called *Viridiplantae*, obtain most of their energy from sunlight via a process called photosynthesis.

Aristotle divided all living things between plants (which generally do not move), and animals (which often are mobile to catch their food). In Linnaeus' system, these became the Kingdoms Vegetabilia (later Metaphyta or Plantae) and Animalia (also called Metazoa). Since then, it has become clear that the Plantae as originally defined included several unrelated groups, and the fungi and several groups of algae were removed to new kingdoms. However, these are still often considered plants in many contexts, both technical and popular.

Most algae are no longer classified within the Kingdom Plantae. The algae comprise several different groups of organisms that produce energy through photosynthesis, each of which arose independently from separate non-photosynthetic ancestors. Most conspicuous among the algae are the seaweeds, multicellular algae that may roughly resemble terrestrial plants, but are classified among the green, red, and brown algae. Each of these algal groups also includes various microscopic and single-celled organisms.

The two groups of green algae are the closest relatives of land plants (embryophytes). The first of these groups is the Charophyta (desmids and stoneworts), from which the embryophytes developed. The sister group to the combined embryophytes and charophytes is the other group of green algae,Chlorophyta, and this more inclusive group is collectively referred to as the green plants or Viridiplantae. The Kingdom Plantae is often taken to mean this monophyletic grouping. With a few exceptions among the green algae, all such forms have cell walls containing cellulose, have chloroplasts containing chlorophylls *a* and *b*, and store food in the form of starch. They undergo closed mitosis without centrioles, and typically have mitochondria with flat cristae.

The chloroplasts of green plants are surrounded by two membranes, suggesting they originated directly from endosymbiotic cyanobacteria. The same is true of two additional groups of algae: the Rhodophyta (red algae) and Glaucophyta. All three groups together are generally believed to have a common origin, and so are classified together in the taxon Archaeplastida. In contrast, most other algae (e.g. heterokonts, haptophytes, dinoflagellates, and euglenids) have chloroplasts with three or four surrounding membranes. They are not close relatives of the green plants, presumably acquiring chloroplasts separately from ingested or symbiotic green and red algae.

Fungi were previously included in the plant kingdom, but are now seen to be more closely related to animals. Unlike embryophytes and algae which are generally photosynthetic, fungi are often saprotrophs: obtaining food by breaking down and absorbing surrounding materials. Most fungi are formed by microscopic structures called hyphae, which may or may not be divided into cells but contain eukaryotic nuclei. Fruiting bodies, of which mushrooms are most familiar, are the reproductive structures of fungi. They are not related to any of the photosynthetic groups, but are close relatives of animals. Therefore, the fungi are in a kingdom of their own.

The plants that are likely most familiar to us are the multicellular land plants, called embryophytes. They include the vascular plants, plants with full systems of leaves, stems, and roots. They also include a few of their close relatives, often called *bryophytes*, of which mosses and liverworts are the most common.

All of these plants have eukaryotic cells with cell walls composed of cellulose, and most obtain their energy through photosynthesis, using light and carbon dioxide to synthesize food. About three hundred plant species do not photosynthesize but are parasites on other species of photosynthetic plants. Plants are distinguished from green algae, which represent a mode of photosynthetic life similar to the kind modern plants are believed to have evolved from, by having specialized reproductive organs protected by non-reproductive tissues.

Bryophytes first appeared during the early Paleozoic. They can only survive where moisture is available for significant periods, although some species are desiccation tolerant. Most species of bryophyte remain small throughout their life-cycle. This involves an alternation between two generations: a haploid stage, called the gametophyte, and a diploid stage, called the sporophyte. The sporophyte is short-lived and remains dependent on its parent gametophyte.

Vascular plants first appeared during the Silurian period, and by the Devonian had diversified and spread into many different land environments. They have a number of adaptations that allowed them to overcome the limitations of the bryophytes. These include a cuticle resistant to desiccation, and vascular tissues which transport water throughout the organism. In most the sporophyte acts as a separate individual, while the gametophyte remains small.

The first primitive seed plants, Pteridosperms (seed ferns) and Cordaites, both groups now extinct, appeared in the late Devonian and diversified through the Carboniferous, with further evolution through the Permian and Triassic periods. In these the gametophyte stage is completely reduced, and the sporophyte begins life inside an enclosure called a seed, which develops while on the parent plant, and with fertilisation by means of pollen grains. Whereas other vascular plants, such as ferns, reproduce by means of spores and so need moisture to develop, some seed plants can survive and reproduce in extremely arid conditions.

Early seed plants are referred to as gymnosperms (naked seeds), as the seed embryo is not enclosed in a protective structure at pollination, with the pollen landing directly on the embryo. Four surviving groups remain widespread now, particularly the conifers, which are dominant trees in several biomes. The angiosperms, comprising the flowering plants, were the last major group of plants to appear, emerging from within the gymnosperms during the Jurassic and diversifying rapidly during the Cretaceous. These differ in that the seed embryo (angiosperm) is enclosed, so the pollen has to grow a tube to penetrate the protective seed coat; they are the predominant group of flora in most biomes today.

Plant fossils include roots, wood, leaves, seeds, fruit, pollen, spores, phytoliths, and amber (the fossilized resin produced by some plants). Fossil land plants are recorded in terrestrial, lacustrine, fluvial and nearshore marine sediments. Pollen, spores and algae (dinoflagellates and acritarchs) are used for dating sedimentary rock sequences. The remains of fossil plants are not as common as fossil animals, although plant fossils are locally abundant in many regions worldwide.

The earliest fossils clearly assignable to Kingdom Plantae are fossil green algae from the Cambrian. These fossils resemble calcified multicellular members of the Dasycladales. Earlier Precambrian fossils are known which resemble single-cell green algae, but definitive identity with that group of algae is uncertain.

The oldest known fossils of embryophytes date from the Ordovician, though such fossils are fragmentary. By the Silurian, fossils of whole plants are preserved, including the lycophyte *Baragwanathia longifolia.* From the Devonian, detailed fossils of rhyniophytes have been found. Early fossils of these ancient plants show the individual cells within the plant tissue. The Devonian period also saw the evolution of what many believe to be the first modern tree, *Archaeopteris.* This fern-like tree combined a woody trunk with the fronds of a fern, but produced no seeds.

The Coal measures are a major source of Paleozoic plant fossils, with many groups of plants in existence at this time. The spoil heaps of coal mines are the best places to collect; coal itself is the remains of fossilised plants, though structural detail of the plant fossils is rarely visible in coal. In the Fossil Forest at Victoria Park in Glasgow, Scotland, the stumps of *Lepidodendron* trees are found in their original growth positions.

The fossilized remains of conifer and angiosperm roots, stems and branches may be locally abundant in lake and inshore sedimentary rocks from the Mesozoic and Cenozoic eras. Sequoia and its allies, magnolia, oak, and palms are often found.

Petrified wood is common in some parts of the world, and is most frequently found in arid or desert areas where it is more readily exposed by erosion. Petrified wood is often heavily silicified (the organic material replaced by silicon dioxide), and the impregnated tissue is often preserved in fine detail. Such specimens may be cut and polished using lapidary equipment. Fossil forests of petrified wood have been found in all continents.

Most of the solid material in a plant is taken from the atmosphere. Through a process known as photosynthesis, most plants use the energy in sunlight to convert carbon dioxide from the atmosphere, plus water, into simple sugars. Parasitic plants, on the other hand, use the resources of its host to grow. These sugars are then used as building blocks and form the main structural component of the plant. Chlorophyll, a green-coloured, magnesium-containing pigment is essential to this process; it is generally present in plant leaves, and often in other plant parts as well.

Plants usually rely on soil primarily for support and water (in quantitative terms), but also obtain compounds of nitrogen, phosphorus, and other crucial elemental nutrients. Epiphytic and lithophytic plants often depend on rainwater or other sources for nutrients and carnivorous plants supplement their nutrient requirements with insect prey that they capture. For the majority of plants to grow successfully they also require oxygen in the atmosphere and around their roots for respiration. However, some plants grow as submerged aquatics, using oxygen dissolved in the surrounding water, and a few specialized vascular plants, such as mangroves, can grow with their roots in anoxic conditions.

Factors Affecting Growth

The genotype of a plant affects its growth, for example selected varieties of wheat grow rapidly, maturing within 110 days, whereas others, in the same environmental conditions, grow more slowly and mature within 155 days.

Growth is also determined by environmental factors, such as temperature, available water, available light, and available nutrients in the soil. Any change in the availability of these external conditions will be reflected in the plants growth.

Biotic factors are also capable of affecting plant growth. Plants compete with other plants for space, water, light and nutrients. Plants can be so crowded that no single individual produces normal growth. Optimal plant growth can be hampered by grazing animals, suboptimal soil composition, lack of mycorrhizal fungi, and attacks by insects or plant diseases, including those caused by bacteria, fungi, viruses, and nematodes.

Simple plants like algae may have short life spans as individuals, but their populations are commonly seasonal. Other plants may be organized according to their seasonal growth pattern: annual plants live and reproduce within one growing season, biennial plants live for two growing seasons and usually reproduce in second year, and perennial plants live for many growing seasons and continue to reproduce once they are mature. These designations often depend on climate and other environmental factors; plants that are annual in alpine or temperate regions can be biennial or perennial in warmer climates. Among the vascular plants, perennials include both evergreens that keep their leaves the entire year, and deciduous plants which lose their leaves for some part of it. In temperate and boreal climates, they generally lose their leaves during the winter; many tropical plants lose their leaves during the dry season.

The growth rate of plants is extremely variable. Some mosses grow less than 0.001 millimeters per hour (mm/h), while most trees grow 0.025-0.250 mm/h. Some climbing species, such as kudzu, which do not need to produce thick supportive tissue, may grow up to 12.5 mm/h.

Plants protect themselves from frost and dehydration stress with antifreeze proteins, heat-shock proteins and sugars (sucrose is common). LEA (Late Embryogenesis Abundant) protein expression is induced by stresses and protects other proteins from aggregation as a result of desiccation and freezing.

Plant cells are typically distinguished by their large water-filled central vacuole, chloroplasts, and rigid cell walls that are made up of cellulose, hemicellulose, and pectin. Cell division is also characterized by the development of a phragmoplast for the construction of a cell plate in the late stages of cytokinesis. Just as in animals, plant cells differentiate and develop into multiple cell types. Totipotent meristematic cells can differentiate into vascular, storage, protective (e.g. epidermal layer), or reproductive tissues, with more primitive plants lacking some tissue types.

Plants are photosynthetic, which means that they manufacture their own food molecules using energy obtained from light. The primary mechanism plants have for capturing light energy is the pigment chlorophyll. All green plants contain two forms of chlorophyll, chlorophyll *a* and chlorophyll *b*. The latter of these pigments is not found in red or brown algae.

Internal Distribution

Vascular plants differ from other plants in that they transport nutrients between different parts through specialized structures, called xylem and phloem. They also have roots for taking up water and minerals. The xylem moves water and minerals from the root to the rest of the plant, and the phloem provides the roots with sugars and other nutrient produced by the leaves.

Ecology

The photosynthesis conducted by land plants and algae is the ultimate source of energy and organic material in nearly all ecosystems. Photosynthesis radically changed the composition of the early Earth's atmosphere, which as a result is now 21 per cent oxygen. Animals and most other organisms are aerobic, relying on oxygen; those that do not are confined to relatively rare anaerobic environments. Plants are the primary producers in most terrestrial ecosystems and form the basis of the food web in those ecosystems. Many animals rely on plants for shelter as well as oxygen and food.

Land plants are key components of the water cycle and several other biogeochemical cycles. Some plants have co-evolved with nitrogen fixing bacteria, making plants an important part of the nitrogen cycle. Plant roots play an essential role in soil development and prevention of soil erosion.

Distribution

Plants are distributed worldwide in varying numbers. While they inhabit a multitude of biomes and ecoregions, few can be found beyond the tundras at the northernmost regions of continental shelves. At the southern extremes, plants have adapted tenaciously to the prevailing conditions.

Plants are often the dominant physical and structural component of habitats where they occur. Many of the Earth's biomes are named for the type of vegetation because plants are the dominant organisms in those biomes, such as grasslands and forests.

Ecological Relationships

Numerous animals have co-evolved with plants. Many animals pollinate flowers in exchange for food in the form of pollen or nectar. Many animals disperse seeds, often by eating fruit and passing the seeds in their feces. Myrmecophytes are plants that have co-evolved with ants. The plant provides a home, and sometimes food, for the ants. In exchange, the ants defend the plant from herbivores and sometimes competing plants. Ant wastes provide organic fertilizer.

The majority of plant species have various kinds of fungi associated with their root systems in a kind of mutualistic symbiosis known as mycorrhiza. The fungi help the plants gain water and mineral nutrients from the soil, while the plant gives the fungi carbohydrates manufactured in photosynthesis. Some plants serve as homes for endophytic fungi that protect the plant from herbivores by producing toxins. The fungal endophyte, *Neotyphodium coenophialum*, in tall fescue (*Festuca arundinacea*) does tremendous economic damage to the cattle industry in the U.S.

Various forms of parasitism are also fairly common among plants, from the semi-parasitic mistletoe that merely takes some nutrients from its host, but still has photosynthetic leaves, to the fully parasitic broomrape and toothwort that acquire all their nutrients through connections to the roots of other plants, and so have no chlorophyll. Some plants, known as myco-heterotrophs, parasitize mycorrhizal fungi, and hence act as epiparasites on other plants.

Many plants are epiphytes, meaning they grow on other plants, usually trees, without parasitizing them. Epiphytes may indirectly harm their host plant by intercepting mineral nutrients and light that the host would otherwise receive. The weight of large numbers of epiphytes may break tree limbs. Hemiepiphytes like the strangler fig begin as epiphytes but eventually set their own roots and overpower and kill their host. Many orchids, bromeliads, ferns and mosses often grow as epiphytes. Bromeliad epiphytes accumulate water in leaf axils to form phytotelmata, complex aquatic food webs.

Approximately 630 plants are carnivorous, such as the Venus Flytrap (*Dionaea muscipula*) and sundew (*Drosera* species). They trap small animals and digest them to obtain mineral nutrients, especially nitrogen and phosphorus.

Importance

The study of plant uses by people is termed economic botany or ethnobotany; some consider economic botany to focus on modern cultivated plants, while ethnobotany focuses on indigenous plants cultivated and used by native peoples. Human cultivation of plants is part of agriculture, which is the basis of human civilization. Plant agriculture is subdivided into agronomy, horticulture and forestry.

Food

Much of human nutrition depends on land plants, either directly or indirectly. Human nutrition depends to a large extent on cereals, especially maize (or corn), wheat and rice. Other staple crops include potato, cassava, and legumes. Human food also includes vegetables, spices, and certain fruits, nuts, herbs, and edible flowers. Beverages produced from plants include coffee, tea, wine, beer and alcohol. Sugar is obtained mainly from sugar cane and sugar beet. Cooking oils and margarine come from maize, soybean, rapeseed, safflower, sunflower, olive and others. Food additives include gum arabic, guar gum, locust bean gum, starch and pectin. Livestock animals including cows, pigs, sheep, and goats are all herbivores; and feed primarily or entirely on cereal plants, particularly grasses.

Wood is used for buildings, furniture, paper, cardboard, musical instruments and sports equipment. Cloth is often made from cotton, flax or synthetic fibers derived from cellulose, such as rayon and acetate. Renewable fuels from plants include firewood, peat and many other biofuels. Coal and petroleum are fossil fuels derived from plants. Medicines derived from plants include aspirin, taxol, morphine, quinine, reserpine, colchicine, digitalis and vincristine. There are hundreds of herbal supplements such as ginkgo, Echinacea, feverfew, and Saint John's wort. Pesticides derived from plants include nicotine, rotenone, strychnine and pyrethrins. Drugs obtained from plants include opium, cocaine and marijuana. Poisons from plants include ricin, hemlock and curare. Plants are the source of many natural products such as fibers, essential oils, dyes, pigments, waxes, tannins, latex, gums, resins, alkaloids, amber and cork. Products derived from plants include soaps, paints, shampoos, perfumes, cosmetics, turpentine, rubber, varnish, lubricants, linoleum, plastics, inks, chewing gum and hemp rope. Plants are also a primary source of basic chemicals for the industrial synthesis of a vast array of organic chemicals. These chemicals are used in a vast variety of studies and experiments.

Aesthetic Uses

Thousands of plant species are cultivated for aesthetic purposes as well as to provide shade, modify temperatures, reduce wind, abate noise, provide privacy, and prevent soil erosion. People use cut flowers, dried flowers and houseplants indoors or in greenhouses. In outdoor gardens, lawn grasses, shade trees, ornamental trees, shrubs, vines, herbaceous perennials and bedding plants are used. Images of plants are often used in art, architecture, humour, language, and photography and on textiles, money, stamps, flags and coats of arms. Living plant art forms include topiary, bonsai, ikebana and espalier. Ornamental plants have sometimes changed the course of history, as in tulipomania. Plants are the basis of a multi-billion dollar per year tourism industry which includes travel to arboretums, botanical gardens, historic gardens, national parks, tulip festivals, rainforests, forests with colourful autumn leaves and the National Cherry Blossom Festival. Venus Flytrap, sensitive plant and resurrection plant are examples of plants sold as novelties.

Scientific and Cultural Uses

Tree rings are an important method of dating in archeology and serve as a record of past climates. Basic biological research has often been done with plants, such as the pea plants used to derive Gregor Mendel's laws of genetics. Space stations or space colonies may one day rely on plants for life support. Plants are used as national and state emblems, including state trees and state flowers. Ancient trees are revered and many are famous. Numerous world records are held by plants. Plants are often used as memorials, gifts and to mark special occasions such as births, deaths, weddings and holidays. Plants figure prominently in mythology, religion and literature. The field of ethnobotany studies plant use by indigenous cultures which helps to conserve endangered species as well as discover new medicinal plants. Gardening is the most popular leisure activity in the U.S. Working with plants or horticulture therapy is beneficial for rehabilitating people with disabilities. Certain plants contain psychotropic chemicals which are extracted and ingested, including tobacco, cannabis (marijuana), and opium.

Negative Effects

Weeds are plants that grow where people do not want them. People have spread plants beyond their native ranges and some of these introduced plants become invasive, damaging existing ecosystems by displacing native species. Invasive plants cause billions of dollars in crop losses annually by displacing crop plants, they increase the cost of production and the use of chemical means to control them affects the environment.

Plants may cause harm to people and animals. Plants that produce windblown pollen invoke allergic reactions in people who suffer from hay fever. A wide variety of plants are poisonous to people and/or animals. Several plants cause skin irritations when touched, such as poison ivy. Certain plants contain psychotropic chemicals, which are extracted and ingested or smoked, including tobacco, cannabis (marijuana), cocaine and opium. Smoking causes damage to health or even death, while some drugs may also be harmful or fatal to people. Both illegal and legal drugs derived from plants may have negative effects on the economy, affecting worker productivity and law enforcement costs. Some plants cause allergic reactions in people and animals when ingested, while other plants cause food intolerances that negatively affect health.

Plant Breeding

Plant breeding is the art and science of changing the genetics of plants for the benefit of humankind . Plant breeding can be accomplished through many different techniques ranging from simply selecting plants with desirable characteristics for propagation, to more complex molecular techniques.

Plant breeding has been practiced for thousands of years, since near the beginning of human civilization. It is now practiced worldwide by individuals such as gardeners and farmers, or by professional plant breeders employed by organizations such as government institutions, universities, crop-specific industry associations or research centres.

International development agencies believe that breeding new crops is important for ensuring food security by developing new varieties that are higher-yielding, resistant to pests and diseases, drought-resistant or regionally adapted to different environments and growing conditions.

Plant breeding in certain situations may lead the domestication of wild plants. Domestication of plants is an artificial selection process conducted by humans to produce plants that have more desirable traits than wild plants, and which renders them dependent on artificial (usually enhanced) environments for their continued existence. The practice is estimated to date back 9,000-11,000 years. Many crops in present day cultivation are the result of domestication in ancient times, about 5,000 years ago in the Old World and 3,000 years ago in the New World. In the Neolithic period, domestication took a minimum of 1,000 years and a maximum of 7,000 years. Today, all of our principal food crops come from domesticated varieties. Almost all the domesticated plants used today for food and agriculture were domesticated in the centres of origin. In these centres there is still a great diversity of closely related wild plants, the so called crop wild relatives that can also be used for improving modern cultivars by plant breeding.

A plant whose origin or selection is due primarily to intentional human activity is called a cultigen, and a cultivated crop species that has evolved from wild populations due to selective pressures from traditional farmers is called a landrace. Landraces, which can be the result of natural forces or domestication, are plants (or animals) that are ideally suited to a particular region or environment. An example are the landraces of rice, *Oryza sativa* subspecies *indica*, which was developed in South Asia, and *Oryza sativa* subspecies *japonica*, which was developed in China.

Classical plant breeding uses deliberate interbreeding (crossing) of closely or distantly related individuals to produce new crop varieties or lines with desirable properties. Plants are crossbred to introduce traits/genes from one variety or line into a new genetic background. For example, a mildew-resistant pea may be crossed with a high-yielding but susceptible pea, the goal of the cross being to introduce mildew resistance without losing the high-yield characteristics. Progeny from the cross would then be crossed with the high-yielding parent to ensure that the progeny were most like the high-yielding parent, (backcrossing). The progeny from that cross would then be tested for yield and mildew resistance and high-yielding resistant plants would be further developed. Plants may also be crossed with themselves to produce inbred varieties for breeding.

Classical breeding relies largely on homologous recombination between chromosomes to generate genetic diversity. The classical plant breeder may also makes use of a number of *in vitro* techniques such as protoplast fusion, embryo rescue or mutagenesis (see below) to generate diversity and produce hybrid plants that would not exist in nature.

The Yecoro wheat (right) cultivar is sensitive to salinity, plants resulting from a hybrid cross with cultivar W4910 (left) show greater tolerance to high salinity.

Traits that breeders have tried to incorporate into crop plants in the last 100 years include:

- Increased quality and yield of the crop
- Increased tolerance of environmental pressures (salinity, extreme temperature, drought)
- Resistance to viruses, fungi and bacteria
- Increased tolerance to insect pests
- Increased tolerance of herbicides

Intraspecific hybridization within a plant species was demonstrated by Charles Darwin and Gregor Mendel, and was further developed by geneticists and plant breeders. In the United Kingdom in the 1880s, it was the pioneering work of Gartons Agricultural Plant Breeders. In the early 20th century, plant breeders realized that Mendel's findings on the non-random nature of inheritance could be applied to seedling populations produced through deliberate pollinations to predict the frequencies of different types.

In 1908, George Harrison Shull described heterosis, also known as hybrid vigor. Heterosis describes the tendency of the progeny of a specific cross to outperform both parents. The detection of the usefulness of heterosis for plant breeding has led to the development of inbred lines that reveal a heterotic yield advantage when they are crossed. Maize was the first species where heterosis was widely used to produce hybrids.

By the 1920s, statistical methods were developed to analyze gene action and distinguish heritable variation from variation caused by environment. In 1933, another important breeding technique, cytoplasmic male sterility (CMS), developed in maize, was described by Marcus Morton Rhoades. CMS is a maternally inherited trait that makes the plant produce sterile pollen. This enables the production of hybrids without the need for labour intensive detasseling.

These early breeding techniques resulted in large yield increase in the United States in the early 20th century. Similar yield increases were not produced elsewhere until after World War II, the Green Revolution increased crop production in the developing world in the 1960s.

After Second World War

Following Second World War a number of techniques were developed that allowed plant breeders to hybridize distantly related species, and artificially induce genetic diversity.

When distantly related species are crossed, plant breeders make use of a number of plant tissue culture techniques to produce progeny from otherwise fruitless mating. Interspecific and intergeneric hybrids are produced from a cross of related species or genera that do not normally sexually reproduce with each other. These crosses are referred to as *wide crosses*. For example, the cereal triticale is a wheat and rye hybrid. The cells in the plants derived from the first generation created from the cross contained an uneven number of chromosomes and as result was sterile. The cell division inhibitor colchicine was used to double the number of chromosomes in the cell and thus allow the production of a fertile line.

Failure to produce a hybrid may be due to pre- or post-fertilization incompatibility. If fertilization is possible between two species or genera, the hybrid embryo may abort before maturation. If this does occur the embryo resulting from an interspecific or intergeneric cross can sometimes be rescued and cultured to produce a whole plant. Such a method is referred to as *embryo rescue.* This technique has been used to produce new rice for Africa, an interspecific cross of Asian rice *(Oryza sativa)* and African rice *(Oryza glaberrima).*

Hybrids may also be produced by a technique called *protoplast fusion.* In this case protoplasts are fused, usually in an electric field. Viable recombinants can be regenerated in culture.

Chemical mutagens like EMS and DMS, radiation and transposons are used to generate mutants with desirable traits to be bred with other cultivars — a process known as *Mutation Breeding.* Classical plant breeders also generate genetic diversity within a species by exploiting a process called somaclonal variation, which occurs in plants produced from tissue culture, particularly plants derived from callus. Induced polyploidy, and the addition or removal of chromosomes using a technique called chromosome engineering may also be used.

When a desirable trait has been bred into a species, a number of crosses to the favoured parent are made to make the new plant as similar to the favoured parent as possible. Returning to the example of the mildew resistant pea being crossed with a high-yielding but susceptible pea, to make the mildew resistant progeny of the cross most like the high-yielding parent, the progeny will be crossed back to that parent for several generations. This process removes most of the genetic contribution of the mildew resistant parent. Classical breeding is therefore a cyclical process.

It should be noted that with classical breeding techniques, the breeder does not know exactly what genes have been introduced to the new cultivars. Some scientists therefore argue that plants produced by classical breeding methods should undergo the same safety testing regime as genetically modified plants. There have been instances where plants bred using classical techniques have been unsuitable for human consumption, for example the poison solanine was unintentionally increased to unacceptable levels in certain varieties of potato through plant breeding. New potato varieties are often screened for solanine levels before reaching the marketplace.

Modern Plant Breeding

Modern plant breeding uses techniques of molecular biology to select, or in the case of genetic modification, to insert, desirable traits into plants.

The following are the major activities of plant breeding:

- Creation of variation
- Selection
- Evaluation
- Release
- Multiplication
- Distribution of the new variety

Marker Assisted Selection

Sometimes many different genes can influence a desirable trait in plant breeding. The use of tools such as molecular markers or DNA fingerprinting can map thousands of genes. This allows plant breeders to screen large populations of plants for those that possess the trait of interest. The screening is based on the presence or absence of a certain gene as determined by laboratory procedures, rather than on the visual identification of the expressed trait in the plant.

A method for efficiently producing homozygous plants from a heterozygous starting plant, which has all desirable traits. This starting plant is induced to produce doubled haploid from haploid cells, and later on creating homozygous/doubled haploid plants from those cells. While in natural offspring recombination occurs and traits can be unlinked from each other, in doubled haploid cells and in the resulting DH plants recombination is no longer an issue. There, a recombination between two corresponding chromosomes does not lead to un-linkage of alleles or traits, since it just leads to recombination with its identical copy. Thus, traits on one chromosome stay linked. Selecting those offspring having the desired set of chromosomes and crossing them will result in a final F1 hybrid plant, having exactly the same set of chromosomes, genes and traits as the starting hybrid plant. The homozygous parental lines can reconstitute the original heterozygous plant by crossing, if desired even in a large quantity. An individual heterozygous plant can be converted into a heterozygous variety (F1 hybrid) without the necessity of vegetative propagation but as the result of the cross of two homozygous/doubled haploid lines derived from the originally selected plant.

Genetic Modification

Genetic modification of plants is achieved by adding a specific gene or genes to a plant, or by knocking down a gene with RNAi, to produce a desirable phenotype. The plants resulting from adding a gene are often referred to as transgenic plants. If for genetic modification genes of the species or of a crossable plant are used under control of their native promoter, then they are called cisgenic plants. Genetic modification can produce a plant with the desired trait or traits faster than classical breeding because the majority of the plant's genome is not altered.

To genetically modify a plant, a genetic construct must be designed so that the gene to be added or removed will be expressed by the plant. To do this, a promoter to drive transcription and a termination sequence to stop transcription of the new gene, and the gene or genes of interest must be introduced to the plant. A marker for the selection of transformed plants is also included. In the laboratory, antibiotic resistance is a commonly used marker: plants that have been successfully transformed will grow on media containing antibiotics; plants that have not been transformed will die. In some instances markers for selection are removed by backcrossing with the parent plant prior to commercial release.

The construct can be inserted in the plant genome by genetic recombination using the bacteria *Agrobacterium tumefaciens* or *A. rhizogenes*, or by direct methods like the gene gun or microinjection. Using plant viruses to insert genetic constructs into plants is also a possibility, but the technique is limited by the host range of the virus. For example, Cauliflower mosaic virus (CaMV) only infects cauliflower and related species. Another limitation of viral vectors is that the virus is not usually passed on the progeny, so every plant has to be inoculated.

The majority of commercially released transgenic plants are currently limited to plants that have introduced resistance to insect pests and herbicides. Insect resistance is achieved through incorporation of a gene from *Bacillus thuringiensis* (Bt) that encodes a protein that is toxic to some insects. For example, the cotton bollworm, a common cotton pest, feeds on Bt cotton it will ingest the toxin and die. Herbicides usually work by binding to certain plant enzymes and inhibiting their action. The enzymes that the herbicide inhibits are known as the herbicides *target site*. Herbicide resistance can be engineered into crops by expressing a version of *target site* protein that is not inhibited by the herbicide. This is the method used to produce glyphosate resistant crop plants.

Genetic modification of plants that can produce pharmaceuticals (and industrial chemicals), sometimes called *pharmacrops*, is a rather radical new area of plant breeding.

Issues and Concerns

Modern plant breeding, whether classical or through genetic engineering, comes with issues of concern, particularly with regard to food crops. The question of whether breeding can have a negative effect on nutritional value is central in this respect. Although relatively little direct research in this area has been done, there are scientific indications that, by favouring certain aspects of a plant's development, other aspects may be retarded. A study published in the *Journal of the American College of Nutrition* in 2004, entitled *Changes in USDA Food Composition Data for 43 Garden Crops, 1950 to 1999*, compared nutritional analysis of vegetables done in 1950 and in 1999, and found substantial decreases in six of 13 nutrients measured, including 6 per cent of protein and 38 per cent of riboflavin. Reductions in calcium, phosphorus, iron and ascorbic acid were also found. The study, conducted at the Biochemical Institute, University of Texas at Austin, concluded in summary: *"We suggest that any real declines are generally most easily explained by changes in cultivated varieties between 1950 and 1999, in which there may be trade-offs between yield and nutrient content."*

The debate surrounding genetically modified food during the 1990s peaked in 1999 in terms of media coverage and risk perception, and continues today — for example, "*Germany has thrown its weight behind a growing European mutiny over genetically modified crops by banning the planting of a widely grown pest-resistant corn variety.*" The debate encompasses the ecological impact of genetically modified plants, the safety of genetically modified food and concepts used for safety evaluation like substantial equivalence. Such concerns are not new to plant breeding. Most countries have regulatory processes in place to help ensure that new crop varieties entering the marketplace are both safe and meet farmers' needs. Examples include variety registration, seed schemes, regulatory authorizations for GM plants, etc.

Plant breeders' rights is also a major and controversial issue. Today, production of new varieties is dominated by commercial plant breeders, who seek to protect their work and collect royalties through national and international agreements based in intellectual property rights. The range of related issues is complex. In the simplest terms, critics of the increasingly restrictive regulations argue that, through a combination of technical and economic pressures, commercial breeders are reducing biodiversity and significantly constraining individuals (such as farmers) from developing and trading seed on a regional level . Efforts to strengthen breeders' rights, for example, by lengthening periods of variety protection, are ongoing.

When new plant breeds or cultivars are bred, they must be maintained and propagated. Some plants are propagated by asexual means while others are propagated by seeds. Seed propagated cultivars require specific control over seed source and production procedures to maintain the integrity of the plant breeds results. Isolation is necessary to prevent cross contamination with related plants or the mixing of seeds after harvesting. Isolation is normally accomplished by planting distance but in certain crops, plants are enclosed in greenhouses or cages (most commonly used when producing F1 hybrids.)

The development of agricultural science, with phenomenon like the Green Revolution arising, have left millions of farmers in developing countries, most of whom operate small farms under unstable and difficult growing conditions, in a precarious situation. The adoption of new plant varieties by this group has been hampered by the constraints of poverty and the international policies promoting an industrialised model of agriculture. Their response has been the creation of a novel and promising set of research methods collectively known as participatory plant breeding. Participatory means that farmers are more involved in the breeding process and breeding goals are defined by farmers instead of international seed companies with their large-scale breeding programmes. Farmer's groups and NGOs, for example, may wish to affirm local people's rights over genetic resources, produce seeds themselves, build farmers' technical expertise, or develop new products for niche markets, like organically grown food.

House Plant

A *house plant* is a plant that is grown indoors in places such as residences and offices. House plants are commonly grown for decorative purposes and health reasons such as indoor air purification. Plants used in this fashion are most commonly, though not always, tropical or semi-tropical.

Major factors that should be considered when caring for house plants are moisture, light, soil mixture, temperature, humidity, fertilizers, potting, and pest control. The following includes some general guidelines for house plant care. For specific house plant needs, the tags that sometimes come with plants are notoriously unhelpful and generic. Specific care information may be found widely online and in books.

Moisture

Both under-watering and over-watering can be detrimental to a house plant. The best way to determine whether a plant needs water is to check the soil moisture. Feeling the soil is most reliable, since moisture meters are often inaccurate. Most potted plants must be allowed to reach an appropriate level of dryness in between waterings, though the amount of watering required varies greatly depending on the species. Proper soil moisture can range from still slightly moist on the soil surface to very dry to nearly the bottom of the pot. Watering a plant by the calendar is not recommended. If a plant does need to be watered, water should be slowly poured over the surface of the soil until it begins to drain out the bottom of the pot, ensuring complete saturation. However, sometimes the soil separates from the sides of the pot if it is allowed to dry out thoroughly, allowing the water to flow down the sides of the rootball and out the bottom too quickly to be absorbed and retained by the soil and roots. If this is the case, it may be necessary to set the plant in a shallow dish of water long enough for it to soak up enough water to moisten the rootball to its centre. Repotting should eliminate this problem. Repotting should be done only when necessary, since the roots of a plant that is in an excessively large pot may rot.

Light

Through the process of photosynthesis, plants convert the energy in sunlight to chemical energy, which fuels plant growth. The two important factors for providing light to a house plant are *intensity* and *duration*.

Different plants require different light intensities. Intensity (or quality) of light is difficult to measure without a light meter. It is usually measured in units of lux. 100 lux or less is usually considered 'low intensity' or 'indirect' lighting. A bright office has about 400 lux of illumination. 1,000 lux or more is usually considered 'high intensity' lighting. Direct outdoor sunlight is in the range 32,000-100,000 lux. Foot-candles are also occasionally used.

The duration of light exposure is as important as the intensity. Quality exposure of 8 to 16 hours is ideal for most plants. Photoperiodism must also be considered, since some plants such as Poinsettia and Schlumbergera are influenced by either decreasing or increasing daylight hours.

Windows are the most common sources of light for house plants. In the Northern Hemisphere, south-facing windows have the most sun exposure, while western, eastern, and north-facing windows have progressively less exposure. Natural sunlight through windows is affected by seasonal changes, cloud cover, and window treatments. The length of time that light is provided will determine how the plant grows. Providing 16 hours of light/day will promote strong roots, stems and abundant leaves. Decreasing that amount to 12 hours of light/day will signal that the short days of Winter are coming so the plant energy will focus more on flower production and less on green growth.

Artificial light sources can provide an alternative or supplement to window lighting. Fluorescent lighting provides excellent light quality whereas standard incandescent bulbs do little to promote plant growth. 'Cool', or 'blue', fluorescent lights at 6500k provide the light needed for lush green foliage plants, while 'warm', or 'red', fluorescent lights at 3000k provide the light needed for blooming flowers and fruit production. Warm whites are better for flowering plants while cool whites are more suitable for green, leafy growth. When used together, these bulbs are closer to the full spectrum light that comes from the sun, although less powerful.

There are several types of lighting units which can sustain indoor plants. Choosing the best type depends on the need of the plants grown and/or your budget. For the sake of efficiency, incandescents, no matter how cheap, should not be used. Not only do they provide little or no benefit to plants, but the cost of the electricity will outweigh the cost of purchasing multiple incandescent bulbs and fixtures in the long run. Fluorescents are your safest bet. CFL fluorescents are the cheapest option, but more than a couple bulbs are almost always required to be running at once. The next step up is shop lights, available mostly in 2-ft. or 4-ft. fluorescent tubes. The best type of fluorescent are called High Output Fluorescents. Also available in 2-ft and 4-ft. tubes, these bulbs provide more wattage (54 watts each is standard) thus more lumens per watt (92 at the current time). That's about 5,000 lumens per dual 4-ft H.O. Fluorescent Unit. The most serious lights that are used by professionals and in greenhouses as a supplement, are known as Metal Halide or High Pressure Sodium Grow Lights. These lights provide the most lumens, heat and intensity of light so they should be positioned respectively further from the tops of plants to prevent burning.

Soil

House plants are generally grown in specialized soils called *potting compost* or *potting soil*, not in local natural soil. A good potting compost mixture includes soil conditioners to provide the plant with nutrients, support, adequate drainage, and proper aeration. Most potting composts contain a combination of peat and vermiculite or perlite. Concern over environmental damage to peat bogs, however, is leading to the replacement of peat by coir (coconut fibre), which is a sustainable resource. A nutrient rich compost can usually be bought wherever potted plants are sold.

If local natural soil is to be used, it should first be heat sterilized by placing the soil in an oven at 90 °C (200 °F) for at least 30 minutes. This will ensure that the soil does not contain any harmful bacteria. Most locals soils, especially those with a high proportion of clay, do not drain well enough to be a suitable growing medium for house plants. Coir or peat is used to increase aeration and make heavy soils more absorbent. Vermiculite and perlite aid in drainage in a soil mixture. Perlite is recommended over vermiculite because it does not break down as easily. A coarse grade sand or grit can be used as a substitute for a drainage mechanism if needed. These three ingredients can be mixed in varying ratios to create different potting soil types. For a plant that requires fast drainage, such as a cactus, use plenty of coarse sand, grit or perlite. For a plant that requires plenty of moisture, use more coir. A good all purpose soil mixture is 2 parts coir and 1 part perlite or vermiculite. A so-called 'heavy soil mix' will contain sterilised soil, milled sphagnum moss or coir, and perlite in equal proportions. It is also possible to make a soil mixture that actually contains no soil by mixing equal parts peat moss and perlite (or vermiculite). The soiless mixture will retain more moisture.

Temperature

Most house plants are tropical species selected for their adaptation to growth in a climate which ranges from 15 ºC to 25ºC (60ºF to 80ºF), similar to the temperature in most homes. Temperature control for other plants with differing requirements needs attention to heating and/or cooling.

Humidity

Humidity is slightly more difficult to control than temperature. The more commonly used house plants have established that they can survive in low humidity environments as long as their roots are kept properly irrigated. Most plants thrive in 80 per cent relative humidity while most homes are usually kept around 20 per cent to 60 per cent relative humidity. Besides buying a humidifier, there are a few things that can be done to increase humidity around house plants. The most popular methods used to raise the ambient humidity are misting and pebble trays, which are shallow trays covered with pebbles and filled with water that evaporates to increase humidity. Other methods of raising humidity include grouping plants closely together and not placing plants in drafty areas. Misting is somewhat controversial among gardeners, with some that swear by it and others that say it does little to increase humidity around plants.

Fertilizers

In a potted environment, soil nutrients can eventually deplete. Adding fertilizer can artificially provide these nutrients. However, adding unnecessary fertilizer can be harmful to the plant. Because of this, careful consideration must be taken before fertilizing. If a plant has been in the same potting mix for a year or more and is no longer thriving, then it may be a candidate for nutrient replacement done by using a complete fertilizer at half the recommended label dilution rate.

Fertilizers are usually marked with a number such as 20-20-20. These numbers indicate the percentages of nitrogen, phosphorus, and potassium respectively, the three elements that are needed in the most quantity for plant growth. Nitrogen is essential for green, leafy growth. Phosphorous is essential for flowering or fruiting plants. Potassium is essential for strong roots and increased nutrient uptake. Numbers higher than 15 are usually man-made, chemical fertilizers. Organic fertilizers have a much lower ratio. A 4-2-2 ratio of these elements is usually good for green foliage plants, while a 2-6-4 ratio is usually better for flowering plants. A complete fertilizer will also include the minor and trace elements, such as calcium, magnesium and iron.

While variation may occur between brands, a general rule is to mix 1 tablespoon to every gallon of water. In all cases, it is better to under-fertilize than over-fertilize. The diluted mixture is then used to water the plants. The growth of the plants should be monitored to determine if the fertilizer is helping or harming, and how often (if at all) it should be used. Schedules can range from every other week to every three months. For convenience, granular, time-released fertilizers are also available.

Pot Types and Sizes

Proper pot size is an important factor to consider. A pot that is too large will cause root disease because of the excess moisture retained in the soil, while a pot that is too small will restrict a plant's growth. Generally, a plant can stay in the same pot for two or so years. Pots come in a variety of types as well, but usually can be broken down into two groups: porous and non-porous. Porous pots are usually clay and are highly recommended because they provide better aeration as air passes laterally through the sides of the pot. Non-porous pots such as glazed or plastic pots tend to hold moisture longer and restrict airflow. Another needed feature is drainage holes. Usually pots come with holes in the bottom to allow excess water to flow out of the soil which helps to prevent root rot. If a pot does not have drainage holes, it is best to double pot that plant so the inner pot can be lifted out and the excess water accumulated in the bottom of the outer pot can be removed. Soak old pots thoroughly in a solution of 1 part bleach to 10 parts water to kill any bacteria that may remain.

Effect on Indoor Air Pollution

Indoor plants reduce components of indoor air pollution, particularly volatile organic compounds (VOC) such as benzene, toluene, and xylene. The compounds are removed primarily by soil microorganisms. Plants can also remove CO2, which is correlated with lower work performance, from indoor areas. The effect has been investigated by NASA for use in spacecrafts. Plants also appear to reduce airborne microbes and increase humidity. Certain plants, such as the clivia miniata are able to attract dust particles to their leaves.

Aglaonema (Chinese Evergreen) *Amaryllis Aphelandra squarrosa* (Zebra Plant) *Araucaria heterophylla* (Norfolk Island Pine) *Asparagus densiflorus* (Asparagus Fern) *Begonia* species and cultivars *Bromeliaceae* (Bromeliads) *Chamaedorea elegans* (Parlor Palm) *Chlorophytum comosum* (Spider Plant) *Citrus*, compact cultivars such as the Meyer Lemon *Dracaena Dieffenbachia* (Dumbcane) *Epipremnum aureum* (Golden Pothos) *Ficus benjamina* (Weeping Fig) *Ficus elastica* (Rubber Plant) *Hippeastrum Mimosa pudica* (Sensitive Plant) *Nephrolepis exaltata cv. Bostoniensis* (Boston Fern) *Orchidaceae* (The orchids).

Cattleya and intergeneric hybrids thereof (e.g. Brassolaeliocattleya, Sophrolaeliocattleya)

- *Cymbidium*
- *Dendrobium*
- *Miltoniopsis*
- *Oncidium*
- *Paphiopedilum*
- *Phalaenopsis*
- *Peperomia* species
- *Philodendron* species
- *Maranta* (The Prayer Plants)
- *Saintpaulia* (African violet)
- *Sansevieria trifasciata* (Mother-inlaw's tongue)
- *Schefflera arboricola* (Umbrella Plant)
- *Sinningia speciosa* (Gloxinia)
- *Spathiphyllum* (Peace Lily)
- *Stephanotis floribunda* (Madagascar Jasmine)
- *Tradescantia zebrina* (Purple Wandering Jew)

Succulents

- *Aloe vera*
- Cactaceae (Cacti)
- *Epiphyllum* (Orchid Cacti)
- *Mammillaria*
- *Opuntia* (Large genus that includes the Prickly Pear)
- *Zygocactus* (Christmas Cactus)
- *Crassula ovata* (Jade Plant)

Forced Bulbs

- *Crocus*
- *Hyacinthus* (Hyacinth)

Gardening

Gardening is the practice of growing plants. Ornamental plants are normally grown for their flowers, foliage, overall appearance, or for their dyes. Useful plants are grown for consumption (vegetables, fruits, herbs, and leaf vegetables) or for medicinal use. A *gardener* is someone who practices gardening.

Gardening ranges in scale from fruit orchards, to long boulevard plantings with one or more different types of shrubs, trees and herbaceous plants, to residential yards including lawns and foundation plantings, to large or small containers grown inside or outside. Gardening may be very specialized, with only one type of plant grown, or involve a large number of different plants in mixed plantings. It involves an active participation in the growing of plants, and tends to be labour intensive, which differentiates it from farming or forestry.

Gardening for food extends far back into prehistory. Ornamental gardens were known in ancient times, a famous example being the Hanging Gardens of Babylon, while ancient Rome had dozens of gardens.

Residential gardening takes place near the home, in a space referred to as the *garden*. Although a garden typically

Flowers of *Malus Sylvestris* (Crab Apple)

A Eucalyptus Plantation

Flower Garden

Newly Grafted Cherry Tree, Tape has been used to bind the rootstock and scion at the graft and tar paint to protect the cut end of the scion from desiccation. The buds will burst within the next few weeks to produce leaves and shoots

Husband and Wife Tree — Natural Grafting in Blackthorn Prunus Spinosa

Hybrid Tomatoes Growth by Hydroponic Methods on Straw Bales

Ginkgos along Harlem Avenue in Riverside Illinois

Beech Leaves

An Arborist using a Chainsaw to Fell a Eucalyptus Tree in a Public Park

is located on the land near a residence, it may also be located on a roof, in an atrium, on a balcony, in a windowbox, or on a patio or vivarium.

Gardening also takes place in non-residential green areas, such as parks, public or semi-public gardens (botanical gardens or zoological gardens), amusement and amusement parks, along transportation corridors, and around tourist attractions and garden hotels. In these situations, a staff of gardeners or groundskeepers maintains the gardens.

- Indoor gardening is concerned with the growing of houseplants within a residence or building, in a conservatory, or in a greenhouse. Indoor gardens are sometimes incorporated as part of air conditioning or heating systems.
- Native plant gardening is concerned with the use of native plants with or without the intent of creating wildlife habitat. The goal is to create a garden in harmony with, and adapted to a given area. This type of gardening typically reduces water usage, maintenance, and fertilization costs, while increasing native faunal interest.
- Water gardening is concerned with growing plants adapted to pools and ponds. Bog gardens are also considered a type of water garden. These all require special conditions and considerations. A simple water garden may consist solely of a tub containing the water and plant(s). In aquascaping, a garden is created within an aquarium tank.
- Container gardening is concerned with growing plants in any type of container either indoors or outdoors. Common containers are pots, hanging baskets, and planters. Container gardening is usually used in atriums and on balconies, patios, and roof tops.

Community gardening is a social activity in which an area of land is gardened by a group of people, providing access to fresh produce and plants as well as access to satisfying labour, neighbourhood improvement, sense of community and connection to the environment. Community gardens are typically owned in trust by local governments or non-profits.

Garden sharing partners landowners with gardeners in need of land. These shared gardens, typically front or backyards, are usually used to produce food that is divided between the two parties.

A 'gardener' is any person involved in gardening, arguably the oldest occupation, from the hobbyist in a residential garden, the homeowner supplementing the family food with a small vegetable garden or orchard, to an employee in a plant nursery or the head gardener in a large estate.

The term gardener is also used to describe garden designers and landscape gardeners, who are involved chiefly in the design of gardens, rather than the practical aspects of horticulture.

Gardening Departments and Centres

Gardening departments and centres mainly sell plants, sundries, and garden accessories, but in recent times, many now stock outdoor leisure products as diverse as spas, furniture, and barbecues. Many garden centres now include food halls, and sections for clothing, gifts, pets, and power tools. There are also a number of online garden centres that now deliver direct to customers' doors.

Comparison with Farming

In respect to its food producing purpose, gardening is distinguished from farming chiefly by scale and intent. Farming occurs on a larger scale, and with the production of saleable goods as a major motivation. Gardening is done on a smaller scale, primarily for pleasure and to produce goods for the gardener's own family or community. There is some overlap between the terms, particularly in that some moderate-sized vegetable growing concerns, often called market gardening, can fit in either category.

The key distinction between gardening and farming is essentially one of scale; gardening can be a hobby or an income supplement, but farming is generally understood as a full-time or commercial activity, usually involving more land and quite different practices. One distinction is that gardening is labor-intensive and employs very little infrastructural capital, sometimes no more than a few tools, e.g. a spade, hoe, basket and watering can. By contrast, larger-scale farming often involves irrigation systems, chemical fertilizers and harvesters or at least ladders, e.g. to reach up into fruit trees. However, this distinction is becoming blurred with the increasing use of power tools in even small gardens.

In part because of labour intensity and aesthetic motivations, gardening is very often much more productive per unit of land than farming. In the Soviet Union, half the food supply came from small peasants' garden plots on the huge government-run collective farms, although they were tiny patches of land. Some argue this as evidence of superiority of capitalism, since the peasants were generally able to sell their produce. Others consider it to be evidence of a tragedy of the commons, since the large collective plots were often neglected, or fertilizers or water redirected to the private gardens.

The term precision agriculture is sometimes used to describe gardening using intermediate technology (more than tools, less than harvesters), especially of organic varieties. Gardening is effectively scaled up to feed entire villages of over 100 people from specialized plots. A variant is the community garden which offers plots to urban dwellers; see further in allotment (gardening).Garden design is considered to be an art in most cultures, distinguished from gardening, which generally means *garden maintenance.* In Japan, Samurai and Zen monks were often required to build decorative gardens or practice related skills like flower arrangement known as *ikebana.* In 18th century Europe, country estates were refashioned by landscape gardeners into formal gardens or landscaped park lands, such as at Versailles, France or Stowe, England. Today, landscape architects and garden designers continue to produce artistically creative designs for private garden spaces.

Professional landscape designers are certified by the Association of Professional Landscape Designers.

Social Aspects

People can express their political or social views in gardens, intentionally or not. The lawn *vs.* garden issue is played out in urban planning as the debate over the 'land ethic' that is to determine urban land use and whether hyper hygienist bylaws (e.g. weed control) should apply, or whether land should generally be allowed to exist in its natural wild state. In a famous Canadian Charter of Rights case, 'Sandra Bell *vs.* City of Toronto', 1997, the right to cultivate all native species, even most varieties deemed noxious or allergenic, was upheld as part of the right of free expression.

People often surround their house and garden with a hedge. Common hedge plants are privet, hawthorn, beech, yew, leyland cypress, hemlock, arborvitae, barberry, box, holly, oleander, forsythia and lavender. The idea of open gardens without hedges may be distasteful to those who enjoy privacy. This may have an advantage to local wildlife by providing a habitat for birds, animals, and wild plants.

The Slow Food movement has sought in some countries to add an edible school yard and garden classrooms to schools, e.g. in Fergus, Ontario, where these were added to a public school to augment the kitchen classroom. Garden sharing, where urban landowners allow gardeners to grow on their property in exchange for a share of the harvest, is associated with the desire to control the quality of one's food, and reconnect with soil and community.

In US and British usage, the production of ornamental plantings around buildings is called *landscaping*, *landscape maintenance* or *grounds keeping*, while international usage uses the term *gardening* for these same activities.

Garden Pests

A garden pest is generally an insect, plant, or animal that engages in activity that the gardener considers undesirable. It may crowd out desirable plants, disturb soil, eat young seedlings, steal fruit, or otherwise kill plants, hamper their growth, damage their appearance, or reduce the quality of the edible or ornamental portions of the plant.

Because each gardener may have different goals, a garden pest is what the gardener considers a pest. For example, *Tropaeolum speciosum*, while beautiful, can be considered a pest if it seeds and starts to grow where it is not wanted. As the root is well below ground, pulling it up does not remove it: it simply grows again and becomes what may be considered a pest.

As another example, in lawns, moss can become dominant and be impossible to eradicate. In some lawns, lichens, especially very damp lawn lichens such as Peltigera lactucfolia and P. membranacea, can become difficult and be considered pests.

There are many ways to remove unwanted pests from a garden. The techniques vary depending on the pest, the gardener's goals, and the gardener's philosophy. For example, snails may be dealt with through a chemical pesticide, an organic pesticide, hand-picking, barriers, or simply growing snail-resistant plants.

Garden

A *garden* is a planned space, usually outdoors, set aside for the display, cultivation, and enjoyment of plants and other forms of nature. The garden can incorporate both natural and man-made materials. The most common form is known as a residential garden. Western gardens are almost universally based around plants. Zoos, which display wild animals in simulated natural habitats, were formerly called *zoological gardens*.

The etymology of the word refers to *enclosure*: it is from Middle English *gardin*, from Anglo-French *gardin*, *jardin*, of Germanic origin; akin to Old High German *gart*, an enclosure. The words *yard*, *court*, and Latin *hortus* (meaning 'garden', hence horticulture and orchard), are cognates — all referring to an enclosed space. The term 'garden' in British English refers to an enclosed area of land, usually adjoining a building. This would be referred to as a yard in American English. Some traditional types of eastern gardens, such as Zen gardens, use plants such as parsley. Xeriscape gardens use local native plants that do not require irrigation or extensive use of other resources while still providing the benefits of a garden environment. Gardens may exhibit structural enhancements, sometimes called follies, including water features such as fountains, ponds (with or without fish), waterfalls or creeks, dry creek beds, statuary, arbors, trellises and more. Some gardens are for ornamental purposes only, while some gardens also produce food crops, sometimes in separate areas, or sometimes intermixed with the ornamental plants. Food-producing gardens are distinguished from farms by their smaller scale, more labour-intensive methods, and their purpose (enjoyment of a hobby rather than produce for sale). Flower gardens combine plants of different heights, colours, textures, and fragrances to create interest and delight the senses. Gardening is the activity of growing and maintaining the garden. This work is done by an amateur or professional gardener. A gardener might also work in a non-garden setting, such as a park, a roadside embankment, or other public space. Landscape architecture is a related professional activity with landscape architects tending to specialise in design for public and corporate clients. Garden design is the creation of plans for layout and planting of gardens and landscapes. Garden design may be done by the garden owner themselves, or by professionals. Most professional garden designers are trained in principles of design and in horticulture, and have an expert knowledge and experience of using plants. Some professional garden designers are also landscape architects, a more formal level of training that usually requires an advanced degree and often a state licence. Elements of garden design include the layout of hard landscape, such as paths, rockeries, walls, water features, sitting areas and decking, as well as the plants themselves, with consideration for their horticultural requirements, their season-to-season appearance, lifespan, growth habit, size, speed of growth, and combinations with other plants and landscape features. Consideration is also given to the maintenance needs of the garden, including the time or funds available for regular maintenance, which can affect the choices of plants regarding speed of growth, spreading or self-seeding of the plants, whether annual or perennial, and bloom-time, and many other characteristics.

The most important consideration in any garden design is, how the garden will be used, followed closely by the desired stylistic genres, and the way the garden space will connect to the home or other structures in the surrounding areas. All of these considerations are subject to the limitations of the budget. Budget limitations can be addressed by a simpler garden style with fewer plants and less costly hardscape materials, seeds rather than sod for lawns, and plants that grow quickly; alternately, garden owners may choose to create their garden over time, area by area.

Elements of a Garden

The elements of a garden consist of the following:

- Natural conditions and materials
- Soil
- Rocks
- Light conditions
- Wind
- Precipitation
- Air quality
- Pollution
- Proximity to ocean (salinity)
- Plant materials
- Rain from sky

Man-made elements:

- Terrace, patio, deck
- Paths
- Lighting
- Raised beds
- Outdoor art/sculpture, such as Gazebos and Pergolas
- Pool, water garden, or other water elements such as drainage system

Uses for the Garden Space

A garden can have aesthetic, functional, and recreational uses:

- Cooperation with nature
- Plant cultivation
- Observation of nature
- Bird-and insect-watching

- Reflection on the changing seasons
- Relaxation
- Family dinners on the terrace
- Children playing in the yard
- Reading and relaxing in the hammock
- Maintaining the flowerbeds
- Pottering in the shed
- Basking in warm sunshine
- Escaping oppressive sunlight and heat
- Growing useful produce
- Flowers to cut and bring inside for indoor beauty
- Fresh herbs and vegetables for cooking

Garden Design

Garden design is the art and process of designing and creating plans for layout and planting of gardens and landscapes. Garden design may be done by the garden owner themselves, or by professionals of varying levels of experience and expertise. Most professional garden designers are trained in principles of design and in horticulture, and have an expert knowledge and experience of using plants. Some professional garden designers are also landscape architects, a more formal level of training that usually requires an advanced degree and often a state licence. Many amateur gardeners also attain a high level of experience from extensive hours working in their own gardens, through casual study, serious study in Master Gardener Programmes, or by joining gardening clubs. For examples of the latter see The Gardeners of America/Men's Garden Clubs of America and National Garden Clubs. Many gardeners in the United States join the American Horticultural Society.

Garden owners have shown an increasing interest in garden design during the late twentieth century, both as enthusiasts of gardening as a hobby, as well as an expansion in the use of professional garden designers.

Whether a garden is designed by a professional or an amateur, certain principles form the basis of effective garden design, resulting in the creation of gardens to meet the needs, goals and desires of the users or owners of the gardens.

Elements of garden design include the layout of hard landscape, such as paths, walls, water features, sitting areas and decking; as well as the plants themselves, with consideration for their horticultural requirements, their season-to-season appearance, lifespan, growth habit, size, speed of growth, and combinations with other plants and landscape features. Consideration is also given to the maintenance needs of the garden, including the time or funds available for regular maintenance, which can affect the choices of plants regarding speed of growth, spreading or self-seeding of the plants, whether annual or perennial, and bloom-time, and many other characteristics.

The most important consideration in garden design is how the garden will be used, followed closely by the desired stylistic genres, and the way the garden space will connect to the home or other structures in the surrounding areas. All of these considerations are subject to the limitations of the budgetary concerns for the particular project and time. Budget limitations can be addressed by a simpler more basic garden style with fewer plants and less costly hardscape materials, seeds rather than sod for lawns, and plants that grow quickly; alternately, garden owners may choose to create their garden over time, area by area, putting more into each section than could be handled all at once.

A garden's location has a substantial influence on the garden design. Many of the great gardens of history and today possess a location that is topographically significant and has a suitable microclimate for plants, a well-designed connection to water, and rich soil. However, a good garden design, one that is well-planned and constructed, can increase the value of the garden more than its location.

Soil

The quality of a garden's soil often has a significant influence on the success of the garden. Soil influences the availability of water and nutrients, the activity of beneficial soil organisms, and a wide variety of other factors important to plant growth.

Traditionally, garden soil is improved by amendment, the process of adding beneficial materials to the excavated native subsoil and topsoil. The materials, which may consist of compost, peat, sand, mineral dust, or manure, among others, are mixed with the excavated soil. The amount and type of amendment may depend on the ratio of clay to humus, and on the soil acidity or alkalinity. One source states that, "conditioning the soil thoroughly before planting enables the plants to establish themselves quickly and so play their part in the design."

Recommendations regarding the scope of soil amendment may vary. One rule of thumb suggests that the gardener till and amend an area twice the size high and wide of any plant container.

However, not all gardens are, or should be, amended in this manner. Since "many native plants prefer an impoverished soil, and the closer to their natural habitat they are in the garden, the better". In this case, poor soil is better than a rich soil that has been artificially enriched.

As well, some authorities recommend against the amendment.

Hedges vary their colours throughout the seasons dramatically. Hedges, being strong features in a garden, are often used to divide sections of the garden. However, since they use the moisture and nutrient from the garden soil to grow as well as other plants, they may not be a good choice and may bring a negative effect to the other plants.

Besides the boundaries that are made up of plants like the hedges, walls made up of various materials can be built between regions. There are broadly three types of walling material: stone, either random or coursed, brick, and concrete in its various forms. It is good to determine what colour, size, and texture will be most appropriate for the garden before actually building the wall.

According to Brookes, fencing can offer an alternative solution, is the walls are too solid for the region of the garden. There are several numbers of fence types that can be used for a garden: animal-proof fence for country situations, peep-proof fences for the suburbs, and urban fences that provide shelter from the winds in exposed roof-top gardens and create internal barriers.

Alternative Surfacing

Usually, a smooth expanse of lawn is often considered essential to a garden. However, a textured surface "made up of loose gravel, small pebbles, or wood chips is much more satisfactory visually" than a smooth surface. According to Brookes, creating a relaxed feel to a garden is often done by loose surfacing made up of bark chips, pebbles, gravels; also, the various textures, shapes, sizes, colours, and materials of many different paving elements can contribute to making a garden plan pattern and texture, if they are mixed successfully.

The history of planting design is an aspect of the history of gardening and the history of landscape architecture. Planting in ancient gardens was often a mix of herbs for medicinal use, vegetables for consumption and flowers for decoration. Purely aesthetic planting layouts seem to have developed after the renaissance and are clearly shown in late-renaissance paintings and plans. The designs were geometrical and plants were used to form patterns. In the East, naturalistic planting design originated as early as around 200 B.C. in China. In the West, the arrangement of plants in informal groups developed as part of the landscape garden style and was strongly influenced by the picturesque.

A planting plan gives specific instructions, often for a contractor about how the soil is to be prepared, what species are to be planted, what size and spacing is to be used and what maintenance operations are to be carried out under the contract. Owners of private gardens may also use planting plans, not for contractual purposes, as an aid to thinking about a design and as a record of what has been planted. A planting strategy is a long term strategy for the design, establishment and management of different types of vegetation in a landscape or garden.

Planting can be established by directly employed gardeners and horticulturalists or it can be established by a landscape contractor (also known as a landscape gardener). Landscape contractors work to drawings and specifications prepared by garden designers or landscape architects.

Planting Design

Planting design requires design judgement combined with a good level of horticultural, ecological and cultural knowledge. It includes two major systems: formal planting design and naturalistic planting design.

Boundaries

The look of the garden can be influenced strongly by the boundary impinges. Planting can be used to modify the boundary line or a line between an area of rough grass and smooth, depending on the size of the plot. Introducing internal boundaries, perhaps in the form of hedges or group of shrubs, can help break up a garden.

Garden furniture may range from a *patio set* consisting of a table, four or six chairs and a parasol, through benches, swings, various lighting, to stunning artifacts in brutal concrete or weathered oak. Patio heaters, that run on bottled butane or propane, are often used to enable people to sit outside at night or in cold weather. A picnic table, is used for the purpose of eating a meal outdoors such as in a garden.

The materials used to manufacture modern patio furniture include stones, metals, vinyl, plastics, resins, glass, and treated woods.

While sunlight is not always easily controlled by the gardener, it is an important element of garden design. The amount of available light is a critical factor in determining what plants may be grown. Sunlight will, therefore, have a substantial influence on the character of the garden. For example, a rose garden is generally not successful in full shade, while a garden of hostas may not thrive in hot sun. As another example, a vegetable garden may need to be placed in a sunny location, and if that location is not ideal for the overall garden design goals, the designer may need to change other aspects of the garden.

In some cases, the amount of available sunlight can be influenced by the gardener. The location of trees, other shade plants, garden structures, or, when designing an entire property, even buildings, might be selected or changed based on their influence in increasing or reducing the amount of sunlight provided to various areas of the property.

In other cases, the amount of sunlight is not under the gardener's control. Nearby buildings, plants on other properties, or simply the climate of the local area, may limit the available sunlight. Or, substantial changes in the light conditions of the garden may not be within the gardener's means. In this case, it is important to plan a garden that is compatible with the existing light conditions.

Light regulates three major plant processes:

- Photosynthesis;
- Phototropism; and
- Photoperiodism.

Photosynthesis provides the energy required to produce the energy source of plants.

Phototropism is the effect of light on plant growth that causes the plant to grow toward or away from the light. Photoperiodism is a plant's response or capacity to respond to photoperiod, a recurring cycle of light and dark periods of constant length.

Lighting

Garden lighting can be an important aspect of garden design. In most cases, various types of lighting techniques may be classified and defined by heights: safety lighting, uplighting, and downlighting. Safety lighting is the most practical application. However, it is more important to determine the type of lamps and fittings needed to create the desired effects.

A formal garden in the Western gardening tradition is a neat and ordered garden laid out in carefully planned geometric and symmetric lines. Lawns and hedges in a formal garden must always be kept neatly clipped. Trees, shrubs, subshrubs and other foliages are carefully arranged, shaped and continually trimmed. A French garden or Garden à la française, is a specific kind of formal garden, laid out in the manner of André Le Nôtre; it is centred on the façade of a building, with radiating avenues and paths of gravel, lawns, parterres and pools (*bassins*) of reflective water enclosed in geometric shapes by stone coping, with fountains and sculpture.

The simplest formal garden would be a box-trimmed hedge lining or enclosing a carefully laid out flowerbed or garden bed of simple geometric shape, such as a knot garden. The most elaborate formal gardens contain pathways, statuary, fountains and beds on differing levels.

The Garden à la française had its origins in sixteenth-century Italian gardens such as Boboli Gardens behind Palazzo Pitti, Florence, laid out by a series of architect-designers for the Grand Duchess Eleanor of Toledo. The formal parterre of clipped evergreens was transferred to France, where some of the earliest formal parterres were those laid out at Anet. Claude Mollet, the founder of a dynasty of nurserymen-designers that lasted deep into the 18th century, introduced the formal parterre. (See also Gardens of the French Renaissance.)

Formal gardens were a feature of the stately homes of England from the introduction of the parterre at Wilton House in the 1630s until such geometries were swept away by the naturalistic landscape gardens of the 1730s, but perhaps the best-known example of a formal garden of gravel, stone, water, turf and trees with sculpture is at Versailles, which is actually many different gardens, laid out by André Le Nôtre. In the early eighteenth century, the publication of Dezallier d'Argenville, *La théorie et la pratique du jardinage* (1709) was translated into English and German, and was the central document for the later formal gardens of Continental Europe.

Formal gardening in the French manner was reintroduced at the turn of the twentieth century: Beatrix Farrand's formal gardens at Dumbarton Oaks, Washington DC and Achille Duchêne's restored water parterre at Blenheim Palace are examples of the modern formal garden. New York City's Central Park features a formal garden in the Conservatory Garden at the northern sector.

Cottage Garden

A cottage garden uses an informal design, traditional materials, dense plantings, and a mixture of ornamental and edible plants. Cottage gardens go back many centuries, but their popularity grew in 1870s England in response to the more structured English estate gardens that used formal designs and massed colours of brilliant greenhouse annuals. They are more casual by design, depending on grace and charm rather than grandeur and formal structure.

The earliest cottage gardens were far more practical than their modern descendants — with an emphasis on vegetables and herbs, along with some fruit trees, perhaps a beehive, and even livestock. Flowers were used to fill any spaces in between. Over time, flowers became more dominant. Modern day cottage gardens include countless regional and personal variations of the more traditional English cottage garden.

A residential or domestic garden, is the most common form of garden and is generally found in proximity to a residence, such as the front or back garden. The front garden may be a formal and semi-public space and so subject to the constraints of convention and law. While typically found in the yard of the residence, a garden may also be established on a roof, in an atrium, on a balcony, in windowboxes, or on a patio. Residential gardens are typically designed at human scale, as they are most often intended for private use. However, the garden of a great house, castle or a large estate may be larger than a public park in a village, and may produce foodstuffs as well.

Residential gardens may feature specialized gardens, such as those for exhibiting one particular type of plant, or special features, such as rockery or water features. They are also used for growing herbs and vegetables and are thus an important element of sustainability.

Kitchen Garden or Potager

The traditional kitchen garden, also known as a potager, is a seasonally used space separate from the rest of the residential garden — the ornamental plants and lawn areas. Most vegetable gardens are still miniature versions of old family farm plots with square or rectangular beds, but the kitchen garden is different not only in its history, but also its design.

The kitchen garden may be a landscape feature that can be the central feature of an ornamental, all-season landscape, but can be little more than a humble vegetable plot. It is a source of herbs, vegetables, fruits, and flowers, but it is also a structured garden space, a design based on repetitive geometric patterns.

The kitchen garden has year-round visual appeal and can incorporate permanent perennials or woody plantings around (or among) the annual plants.

A Shakespeare garden is a themed garden that cultivates plants mentioned in the works of William Shakespeare. In English-speaking countries, particularly the United States, these are often public gardens associated with parks, universities, and Shakespeare festivals. Shakespeare gardens are sites of cultural, educational, and romantic interest and can be locations for outdoor weddings.

Signs near the plants usually provide relevant quotations. A Shakespeare garden usually includes several dozen species, either in herbaceous profusion or in a geometric layout with boxwood dividers. Typical amenities are walkways and benches and a weather-resistant bust of Shakespeare. Shakespeare gardens may accompany reproductions of Elizabethan architecture. Some Shakespeare gardens also grow species typical of the Elizabethan period but not mentioned in Shakespeare's plays or poetry.

Rock Garden

A rock garden, also known as a rockery or an alpine garden, is a type of garden that features extensive use of rocks or stones, along with plants native to rocky or alpine environments.

The usual form of a rock garden is a pile of rocks, large and small, esthetically arranged, and with small gaps between, where the plants will be rooted. Some rock gardens incorporate bonsai.

Some rock gardens are designed and built to look like natural outcrops of bedrock. Stones are aligned to suggest a bedding plane and plants are often used to conceal the joints between the stones. This type of rockery was popular in Victorian times, often designed and built by professional landscape architects. The same approach is sometimes used in modern campus or commercial landscaping, but can also be applied in smaller private gardens.

The Japanese rock garden, in the west often referred to as *Zen garden*, is a special kind of rock garden with hardly any plants. The Rock Garden is a sculpture garden in Chandigarh, India. Spread over an area of forty-acre (160,000 m^2), it is completely built of industrial and home waste and thrown-away items.

Japanese Garden

Japanese gardens can be found at private homes, in neighbourhood or city parks, and at historical landmarks such as Buddhist temples and old castles. Some of the Japanese gardens most famous in the West, and within Japan as well, are dry gardens or rock gardens, *karesansui*. The tradition of the Tea masters has produced highly refined Japanese gardens of quite another style, evoking rural simplicity. In Japanese culture, garden-making is a high art, intimately related to the linked arts of calligraphy and ink painting. Since the end of the 19th century, Japanese gardens have also been adapted to Western settings. Japanese gardens were developed under the influences of the distinctive and stylized Chinese gardens.

Contemporary Garden

The contemporary style garden has become very popular in the UK in the last 10 years. This is partly due to the increase of modern housing with small gardens as well as the cultural shift towards contemporary design. This style of garden can be defined by the use 'clean' design lines, with focus on hard landscaping materials: stone, hardwood, rendered walls. Planting style is bold but simple with the use of drifts of one or two plants that repeat throughout the design. Grasses are a very popular choice for this style of design. Lighting effects also play an integral role in the modern garden. Subtle lighting effects can be achieved with the use of carefully placed low voltage LED lights incorporated into paving.

Cottage Garden

The *cottage garden* is a distinct style of garden that uses an informal design, traditional materials, dense plantings, and a mixture of ornamental and edible plants. English in origin, the cottage garden depends on grace and charm rather than grandeur and formal structure. Homely and functional gardens connected to working-class cottages go back several centuries, but their reinvention in stylized versions grew in 1870s England, in reaction to the more structured and rigorously maintained English estate gardens that used formal designs and mass plantings of brilliant greenhouse annuals.

The earliest cottage gardens were more practical than their modern descendants — with an emphasis on vegetables and herbs, along with some fruit trees, perhaps a beehive, and even livestock. Flowers were used to fill any spaces in between. Over time, flowers became more dominant. The traditional cottage garden was usually enclosed, perhaps with a rose-bowered gateway. Flowers common to early cottage gardens included hollyhocks, pansies and delphinium, all three essentially nineteenth-century flowers. Others were the old-fashioned roses that bloomed once a year with rich scents, simple flowers like daisies, and flowering herbs. A well-tended topiary of traditional form, perhaps a cone-shape in tiers, or a conventionalised peacock, would be part of the repertory, to which the leisured creators of 'cottage gardens' would add a sun-dial, crazy paving on paths with thyme in the interstices, and a rustic seat, generally missing in the earlier cottage gardens. Over time, even large estate gardens had sections they called 'cottage gardens'.

Modern-day cottage gardens include countless regional and personal variations of the more traditional English cottage garden, and embrace plant materials, such as ornamental grasses or native plants, that were never seen in the rural gardens of cottagers. Traditional roses, with their full fragrance and lush foliage, continue to be a cottage garden mainstay — along with modern disease-resistant varieties that keep the traditional attributes. Informal climbing plants, whether traditional or modern hybrids, are also a common cottage garden plant. Self-sowing annuals and freely spreading perennials continue to find a place in the modern cottage garden, just as they did in the traditional cottager's garden.

Cottage gardens, which emerged in Elizabethan times, appear to have originated as a local source for herbs and fruits. One theory is that they arose out of the Black Death of the 1340s, when the death of so many labourers made land available for small cottages with personal gardens. According to the late nineteenth-century legend of origin, these gardens were originally created by the workers that lived in the cottages of the villages, to provide them with food and herbs, with flowers planted in for decoration. Helen Leach analysed the historical origins of the romanticized cottage garden, subjecting the garden style to rigorous historical analysis, along with the ornamental potager and the herb garden. She concluded that their origins were less in workingmen's gardens in the nineteenth century and more in the leisured classes' discovery of simple hardy plants, in part through the writings of John Claudius Loudon. Loudon helped to design the estate at Great Tew, Oxfordshire, where farm workers were provided with cottages that had architectural quality set in a small garden — about an acre — where they could grow food and keep pigs and chickens.

Authentic gardens of the yeoman cottager would have included a beehive and livestock, and frequently a pig and sty, along with a well. The peasant cottager of mediaeval times was more interested in meat than flowers, with herbs grown for medicinal use rather than for their beauty. By Elizabethan times there was more prosperity, and thus more room to grow flowers. Even the early cottage garden flowers typically had their practical use — violets were spread on the floor (for their pleasant scent and keeping out vermin); calendulas and primroses were both attractive and used in cooking. Others, such as sweet william and hollyhocks were grown entirely for their beauty.

The 'naturalness' of informal design began to be noticed and developed by the British leisured class. Alexander Pope was an early proponent of less formal gardens, calling in a 1713 article for gardens with the 'amiable simplicity of unadourned nature'. Other writers in the 18th century who encouraged less formal, and more natural, gardens included Joseph Addison and Lord Shaftesbury. The evolution of cottage gardens can be followed in the issues of *The Cottage Gardener* (1848-61), edited by George William Johnson, where the emphasis is squarely on the 'florist's flowers', carnations and auriculas in fancy varieties that were originally cultivated as a highly-competitive blue-collar hobby.

William Robinson and Gertrude Jekyll helped to popularize less formal gardens in their many books and magazine articles. Robinson's *The Wild Garden*, published in 1870, contained in the first edition an essay on 'The

Garden of British Wild Flowers', which was eliminated from later editions. In his *The English Flower Garden*, illustrated with cottage gardens from Somerset, Kent and Surrey, he remarked, "One lesson of these little gardens, that are so pretty, is that one can get good effects from simple materials." From the 1890s his lifelong friend Jekyll applied cottage garden principles to more structured designs in even quite large country houses. Her *Colour in the Flower Garden* (1908) is still in print today.

Robinson and Jekyll were part of the Arts and Crafts Movement, a broader movement in art, architecture, and crafts during the late 1800s which advocated a return to the informal planting style derived as much from the Romantic tradition as from the actual English cottage garden. The Arts and Crafts Exhibition of 1888 began a movement toward an idealized natural country garden style. The garden designs of Robinson and Jekyll were often associated with Arts and Crafts style houses. Both were influenced by William Morris, one of the leaders of the Arts and Crafts Movement — Robinson quoted Morris's views condemning carpet bedding; Jekyll shared Morris's mystical view of nature and drew on the floral designs in his textiles for her gardening style. When Morris built his Red House in Kent, it influenced new ideas in architecture and gardening — the 'old-fashioned' garden suddenly became a fashion accessory among the British artistic middle class, and the cottage garden esthetic began to emigrate to America.

In the early twentieth century the term 'cottage garden' might be applied even to as large and sophisticated a garden as Hidcote Manor, which Vita Sackville-West described as "a cottage garden on the most glorified scale" but where the colour harmonies were carefully contrived and controlled, as in the famous 'Red Borders'. Sackville-West had taken similar models for her own 'cottage garden', one of many 'garden rooms' at Sissinghurst Castle — her idea of a cottage garden was a place where "the plants grow in a jumble, flowering shrubs mingled with Roses, herbaceous plants with bulbous subjects, climbers scrambling over hedges, seedlings coming up wherever they have chosen to sow themselves". The cottage garden ideal was also spread by artists such as water-colourist Helen Allingham (1848-1926).

The cottage garden in France is a development of the early twentieth century. Monet's garden at Giverny is a prominent example, a sprawling garden full of varied plantings, rich colours, and water gardens. In modern times, the term 'cottage garden' is used to describe any number of informal garden styles, using design and plants very different from their traditional English cottage garden origins. Examples include regional variations using a grass prairie scheme (in the American midwest) and California chapparal cottage gardens.

Design

While the classic cottage garden is built around a cottage, many cottage-style gardens are created around houses and even estates such as Hidcote Manor, with its more intimate 'garden rooms'. The cottage garden design is based more on principles than formulae: it has an informal look, with a seemingly casual mixture of flowers, herbs, and vegetables often packed into a small area. In spite of their appearances, cottage gardens have a design and formality that help give them their grace and charm. Due to space limitations, they are often in small rectangular plots, with practical functioning paths and hedges or fences. The plants, layout, and materials are chosen to give the impression of casualness and a country feel. Modern cottage gardens frequently use local flowers and materials, rather than those of the traditional cottage garden. What they share with the tradition is the unstudied look, the use of every square inch, and a rich variety of flowers, herbs, and vegetables.

The cottage garden is designed to appear artless, rather than contrived or pretentious. Instead of artistic curves, or grand geometry, there is an artfully designed irregularity. Borders can go right up to the house, lawns are replaced with tufts of grass or flowers, and beds can be as wide as needed. Instead of the discipline of large scale colour schemes, there is the simplicity of harmonious colour combinations between neighbouring plants. The overall appearance can be of "a vegetable garden that has been taken over by flowers." The method of planting closely packed plants was supposed to reduce the amount of weeding and watering required, but planted stone pathways or turf paths, and clipped hedges overgrown with wayward vines, are cottage garden features requiring well-timed maintenance.

Materials

Paths, arbors, and fences use traditional or antique looking materials. Wooden fences and gates, paths covered with locally made bricks or stone, and arbors using natural materials all give a more casual — and less formal — look and feel to a cottage garden. Pots, ornaments, and furniture also use natural looking materials with traditional finishes — everything is chosen to give the impression of an old-fashioned country garden.

Plants

Cottage garden plants are chosen for their old-fashioned and informal appeal. Many modern day gardeners use heirloom or 'old-fashioned' plants and varieties — even though these may not have been authentic or traditional cottage garden plants. In addition, there are modern varieties of flowers that fit into the cottage garden look. For example, modern roses developed by David Austin have been chosen for cottage gardens because of their old-fashioned look (multi-petaled form and rosette-shaped flowers) and fragrance — combined with modern virtues of hardiness, repeat blooming, and disease-resistance. Modern cottage gardens often use native plants and those adapted to the local climate, rather than trying to force traditional English plants to grow in an incompatible environment — though many of the old favourites thrive in cottage gardens throughout the world.

Cottage gardens are always associated with roses: shrub roses, climbing roses, and old garden roses with lush foliage, in contrast to the gangly modern hybrid tea roses. Old cottage garden roses include the Gallica rose, which form dense mounded shrubs 3-4 ft high and wide, with pale pink to purple flowers — with single form to full double form blooms. They are also very fragrant, and include the ancient Apothecary's rose, whose magenta flowers were preserved solely for their fragrance. Another old fragrant cottage garden rose is the Damask rose, which is still grown in Europe for use in perfumes. The damasks grow 6 ft or higher, with gently arching canes that help give an informal look to a garden. Even taller are the Alba roses, which are not always white, and which bloom well even in partial shade.

The Provence rose or *Rosa centifolia* is the full and fat rose made famous by Dutch masters in their seventeenth century paintings. These very fragrant shrub roses grow 5 ft tall and wide, with a floppy habit that is aided by training on an arch or pillar. The centifolia roses have produced many descendants that are also cottage garden favourites, including the moss rose. Unlike most modern hybrids, the older roses bloom on the previous year's wood, so they aren't pruned back severely each year like the modern varieties. Because they don't bloom continuously, like their modern counterparts, they can share their branches with Clematis vines, which use the branches for support. A rose in the cottage garden is not segregated with other roses, with bare earth or mulch underneath — but is casually blended with other flowers, vines, and groundcover.

With the introduction of China roses (*rosa chinensis*) late in the eighteenth century, many hybrids were introduced that had the repeat blooming of the China roses, but maintained the informal old rose shape and flower. These included the Bourbon rose and the Noisette rose, which were added to the rose repertoire of the cottage garden. More recently, hybrid 'English' roses introduced by David Austin have become popular cottage garden-style roses. His shrub roses combine the best traits of modern hybrid tea and floribunda roses, with the old garden roses.

Climbing Plants

Many of the old roses had cultivars that grew very long canes, which could be tied to trellises or against walls. These older varieties are called 'ramblers', rather than 'climbers'. Climbing plants in the traditional cottage garden included European honeysuckle (*Lonicera periclymenum*) and Traveller's Joy (*Clematis vitalba*). The modern cottage garden includes many Clematis hybrids that have the old appeal, with sparse foliage that allows them to grow through roses and trees, and along fences and arbors. There are also many Clematis species used in the modern cottage garden, including *Clematis armandii*, *Clematis chrysocoma*, and *Clematis flammula*. Popular honeysuckles for cottage gardens include Japanese honeysuckle and *Lonicera tragophylla*.

Hedging Plants

In the traditional cottage garden, hedges served as fences on the perimeter to keep out marauding livestock and for privacy, along with other practical uses. Hawthorn leaves made a tasty snack or tea, while the flowers were used for making wine. The fast-growing Elderberry, in addition to creating a hedge, provided berries for food and wine, with the flowers being fried in batter or made into lotions and ointments. The wood had many uses, including toys, pegs, skewers, and fishing poles. Holly was another hedge plant, useful because it quickly spread and self-seeded. Privet was also a convenient and fast growing hedge. Over time, more ornamental and less utilitarian plants became popular cottage garden hedges, including laurel, lilac, snowberry, japonica, and others.

Popular flowers in the traditional cottage garden included florist's flowers which were grown by enthusiasts — such as violets, pinks, and primroses — and those grown with a more practical purpose. For example, the calendula, grown today almost entirely for its bright orange flowers, was primarily valued for eating, for adding colour to butter and cheese, for adding smoothness to soups and stews, and for all kinds of healing salves and preparations. Like many old cottage garden annuals and herbs, it freely self-sowed, making it easier to grow and share. Other popular cottage garden annuals included violets, pansies, stocks, and mignonette.

Perennials were the largest group of traditional cottage garden flowers — those with a long cottage garden history include hollyhocks, carnations, sweet williams, marguerites, marigolds, lilies, peonies, tulips, crocus, daisies, foxglove, monkshood, lavender, campanulas, Solomon's seal, evening primrose, lily-of-the-valley, primrose, cowslips, and many varieties of roses.

Today herbs are typically thought of as culinary plants, but in the traditional cottage garden they were considered to be any plant with household uses. Herbs were used for medicine, toiletries, and cleaning products. Scented herbs would be spread on the floor along with rushes to cover odors. Some herbs were used for dying fabrics. Traditional cottage garden herbs included sage, thyme, southernwood, wormwood, catmint, feverfew, lungwort, soapwort, hyssop, sweet woodruff, and lavender.

Fruits

Fruit in the traditional cottage garden would have included an apple and a pear, for cider and perry, gooseberries and raspberries. The modern cottage garden includes many varieties of ornamental fruit and nut trees, such as crabapple and hazel, along with non-traditional trees like dogwood.

Kitchen Garden

The traditional kitchen garden, also known as a potager, is a space separate from the rest of the residential garden - the ornamental plants and lawn areas. Most vegetable gardens are still miniature versions of old family farm plots, but the kitchen garden is different not only in its history, but also its design.

The kitchen garden may serve as the central feature of an ornamental, all-season landscape, or it may be little more than a humble vegetable plot. It is a source of herbs, vegetables, fruits, and flowers, but it is often also a structured garden space with a design based on repetitive geometric patterns.

The kitchen garden has year-round visual appeal and can incorporate permanent perennials or woody plantings around (or among) the annuals.

A potager is a French term for an ornamental vegetable or kitchen garden. Often flowers (edible and non-edible) and herbs are planted with the vegetables to enhance the garden's beauty. The goal is to make the function of providing food aesthetically pleasing.

Plants are chosen as much for their functionality as for their colour and form. Many are trained to grow upward. A well-designed potager can provide food, cut flowers and herbs for the home with very little maintenance. Potagers can disguise their function of providing for a home in a wide array of forms – from the carefree style of the cottage garden to the formality of a knot garden.

Vegetable Garden

A *vegetable garden* (also known as a *vegetable patch* or *vegetable plot*) is a garden that exists to grow vegetables and other plants useful for human consumption, in contrast to a flower garden that exists for aesthetic purposes. It is a small-scale form of vegetable growing. A vegetable garden typically includes a compost heap, and several plots or divided areas of land, intended to grow one or two types of plant in each plot. It is usually located to the rear of a property in the back garden or back yard. Many families have home kitchen and vegetable gardens that they use to produce food. In World War II, many people had a garden called a 'victory garden' which provided food to families and thus freed up resources for the war effort.

With worsening economic conditions and increased interest in organic and sustainable living, many people are turning to vegetable gardening as a supplement to their family's diet. Food grown in the back yard consumes little if any fuel for shipping or maintenance, and the grower can be sure of what exactly was used to grow it. Organic horticulture, or organic gardening, has become increasingly popular for the modern home gardener.

There are many types of vegetable gardens. The potager, a garden in which vegetables, herbs and flowers are grown together, has become more popular than the more traditional rows or blocks.

The *herb garden* is often a separate space in the garden, devoted to growing a specific group of plants known as herbs. These gardens may be informal patches of plants, or they may be carefully designed, even to the point of arranging and clipping the plants to form specific patterns, as in a knot garden.

Herb gardens may be purely functional, or they may include a blend of functional and ornamental plants. The herbs are usually used to flavour food in cooking, though they may also be used in other ways, such as discouraging pests, providing pleasant scents, or serving medicinal purposes (e.g., a physic garden), among others.

A kitchen garden can be created by planting different herbs in pots or containers, with the added benefit of mobility. Although not all herbs thrive in pots or containers, some herbs do better than others. Mint, is an example of herb that is advisable to keep in a container or it will take over the whole garden.

The culinary use of herbs may result in positive medical side-effects. In addition, plants grown within the garden are sometimes specifically targeted to cure common illnesses or maladies such as colds, headaches, or anxiety. During the medieval period, monks and nuns developed specialist medical knowledge and grew the necessary herbs in specialist gardens. Now, especially due to the increase in popularity of alternative medicine, this usage is heavily increasing. Making a medicinal garden however, requires a great number of plants, one for each malady.

Some popular culinary herbs in temperate climates are to a large extent still the same as in the medieval period.

Examples of herbs used for specific purposes (lists are examples only, and not intended to be complete):

- *Annual culinary herbs:* basil, dill, summer savory
- *Perennial culinary herbs:* mint, rosemary, thyme, tarragon
- *Herbs used for potpourri:* lavender, lemon verbena
- *Herbs used for tea:* mint, lemon verbena, chamomile, bergamot, Hibiscus sabdariffa (for making karkade).
- *Herbs used for other purposes:* stevia for sweetening, feverfew for pest control in the garden.

However, herbs often have multiple purposes. For example, mint may be used for cooking, tea, and pest control.

Vegetable

The noun *vegetable* usually means an edible plant or part of a plant other than a sweet fruit or seed.

However, the word is not scientific, and its meaning is largely based on culinary and cultural tradition. Therefore, the application of the word is somewhat arbitrary and subjective. For example, some people consider mushrooms to be vegetables, while others consider them a separate food category.

Some vegetables can be consumed raw, and some may (or must) be cooked in various ways, most often in non-sweet (savory or salty) dishes. However, a few vegetables are often used in desserts and other sweet dishes, such as rhubarb pies and carrot cakes.

As an adjective, the word *vegetable* is used in scientific and technical contexts with a different and much broader meaning, namely of 'related to plants' in general, edible or not — as in *vegetable matter*, *vegetable kingdom*, *vegetable origin*, etc. The meaning of 'vegetable' as 'plant grown for food' was not established until the 18th century.

There are three definitions relating to fruits and vegetables:

- Fruit (scientific): the ovary of a seed-bearing plant;
- Fruit (culinary): any edible part of a plant with a sweet flavour;
- Vegetable: any edible part of a plant with a savory flavour.

In everyday, grocery-store, culinary language, the words 'fruit' and 'vegetable' are mutually exclusive; plant products that are called fruits are hardly ever classified as vegetables, and vice versa. For scientists, the word 'fruit' has a precise botanical meaning (a part that developed from the ovary of a flowering plant), which is considerably different from its common meaning, and includes many poisonous fruits. While peaches, plums, and oranges are 'fruits' in both senses, many items commonly called 'vegetables' — such as eggplants, bell peppers, and tomatoes — are technically fruits, as are most cereals, as well as some spices like black pepper and chillies. Some plant products, such as corn or peas, may be considered vegetables only while still unripe.

The question of whether the tomato is a fruit or a vegetable found its way into the United States Supreme Court in 1893. The court ruled unanimously in *Nix v. Hedden* that a tomato is correctly identified as, and thus taxed as, a vegetable, for the purposes of the 1883 Tariff Act on imported produce. The court did acknowledge, however, that, botanically speaking, a tomato is a fruit.

Languages other than English often have categories that can be identified with the common English meanings of 'fruit' and 'vegetable', but their precise meaning often depends on local culinary traditions. For example, in Brazil the avocado is traditionally consumed with sugar as a dessert or in milk shakes, and hence regarded as a fruit; whereas in other countries (including Mexico and the United States) it is used in salads and dips, and hence considered a vegetable.

The list of food items called 'vegetable' is quite long, and includes many different parts of plants.

'Vegetable' comes from the Latin *vegetabilis* (animated) and from *vegetare* (enliven), which is derived from *vegetus* (active), in reference to the process of a plant growing. This in turn derives from the Proto-Indo-European base **weg-* or **wog-*, which is also the source of the English *wake*, meaning 'become (or stay) alert'.

The word 'vegetable' was first recorded in English in the 15th century, but applied to any plant. This is still the sense of the adjective 'vegetable' in science. The related term vegetation also has a similarly broad scope.

Nutrition

Vegetables are eaten in a variety of ways, as part of main meals and as snacks. The nutritional content of vegetables varies considerably, though generally they contain little protein or fat, and varying proportions of vitamins, pro-vitamins, dietary minerals, fiber and carbohydrates. Vegetables contain a great variety of other phytochemicals, some of which have been claimed to have antioxidant, antibacterial, antifungal, antiviral and anticarcinogenic properties.

However, vegetables often also contain toxins and antinutrients such as a-solanine, a-chaconine, enzyme inhibitors (of cholinesterase, protease, amylase, etc.), cyanide and cyanide precursors, oxalic acid, and more. Depending on the concentration, such compounds may reduce the edibility, nutritional value, and health benefits of dietary vegetables. Cooking and/or other processing may be necessary to eliminate or reduce them.

Colour Pigments

The green colour of leafy vegetables is due to the presence of the green pigment chlorophyll. Chlorophyll is affected by pH and changes to olive green in acid conditions, and bright green in alkaline conditions. Some of the acids are released in steam during cooking, particularly if cooked without a cover.

The yellow/orange colours of fruits and vegetables are due to the presence of carotenoids, which are also affected by normal cooking processes or changes in pH.

The red/blue colouring of some fruits and vegetables (e.g. blackberries and red cabbage) are due to anthocyanins, which are sensitive to changes in pH. When pH is neutral, the pigments are purple, when acidic, red, and when alkaline, blue. These pigments are very water soluble.

For food safety, the CDC recommends proper fruit handling and preparation to reduce the risk of food contamination and foodborne illness. Fresh fruits and vegetables should be carefully selected. At the store, they should not be damaged or bruised and pre-cut pieces should be refrigerated or surrounded by ice. All fruits and vegetables should be rinsed before eating. This recommendation also applies to produce with rinds or skins that are not eaten. It should be done just before preparing or eating to avoid premature spoilage. Fruits and vegetables should be kept separate from raw foods like meat, poultry, and seafood, as well as any cooking utensils or surfaces that may have come into contact with them (e.g. cutting boards). Fruits and vegetables, if they are not going to be cooked, should be thrown away if they have touched raw meat, poultry, seafood or eggs. All cut, peeled, or cooked fruits and vegetables should be refrigerated within 2 hours. After a certain time, harmful bacteria may grow on them and increase the risk of foodborne illness.

Storage

Proper post harvest storage aimed at extending and ensuring shelf life is best effected by efficient cold chain application. All vegetables benefit from proper post harvest care.

Many root and non-root vegetables that grow underground can be stored through winter in a root cellar or other similarly cool, dark and dry place to prevent mold, greening and sprouting. Care should be taken in understanding the properties and vulnerabilities of the particular roots to be stored. These vegetables can last through to early spring and be nearly as nutritious as when fresh.

During storage, leafy vegetables lose moisture, and the vitamin C in them degrades rapidly. They should be stored for as short a time as possible in a cool place, in a container or plastic bag.

Fruit

In broad terms, a *fruit* is a structure of a plant that contains its seeds.

The term has different meanings dependent on context. In non-technical usage, such as food preparation, fruit normally means the fleshy seed-associated structures of certain plants that are sweet and edible in the raw state, such as apples, oranges, grapes, strawberries, juniper berries and bananas, or the similar-looking structures in other plants, even if they are non-edible or non-sweet in the raw state, such as lemons and olives. Seed-associated structures that do not fit these informal criteria are usually called by other names, such as vegetables, pods, nut, ears and cones.

In biology (botany), on the other hand, a 'fruit' is a part of a flowering plant that derives from specific tissues of the flower, mainly one or more ovaries. Taken strictly, this definition excludes many structures that are 'fruits' in the common sense of the term, such as those produced by non-flowering plants (like juniper berries, which are the seed-containing female cones of conifers, and fleshy fruit-like growths that develop from other plant tissues close to the fruit (*accessory fruit*, or more rarely *false fruit* or *pseudocarp*), such as cashew fruits. Often the botanical fruit is only part of the common fruit, or is merely adjacent to it. On the other hand, the botanical sense includes many structures that are not commonly called 'fruits', such as bean pods, corn kernels, wheat grains, tomatoes, and many more. However, there are several variants of the biological definition of fruit that emphasize different aspects of the enormous variety that is found among plant fruits.

Fruits (in either sense of the word) are the means by which many plants disseminate seeds. Most edible fruits, in particular, were evolved by plants in order to exploit animals as a means for seed dispersal; and many animals (including humans to some extent) have become dependent on fruits as a source of food. Fruits account for a substantial fraction of world's agricultural output, and some (such as the apple and the pomegranate) have acquired extensive cultural and symbolic meanings.

Many true fruits, in a botanical sense, are treated as vegetables in cooking and food preparation because they are not sweet. These culinary vegetables include cucurbits (e.g., squash, pumpkin, and cucumber), tomatoes, peas, beans, corn, eggplant, and sweet pepper; some spices, such as allspice and chilies, are botanical fruits. Occasionally, a culinary 'fruit' is not a true fruit in the botanical sense. For example, rhubarb is often referred to as a fruit, because it is used to make sweet desserts such as pies, though only the petiole of the rhubarb plant is edible. In the culinary sense, a fruit is usually any sweet tasting plant product associated with seed(s), a vegetable is any savoury or less sweet plant product, and a nut is any hard, oily, and shelled plant product.

Technically, a cereal grain is a fruit termed a caryopsis. However, the fruit wall is very thin and fused to the seed coat so almost all of the edible grain is actually a seed. Therefore, cereal grains, such as corn, wheat and rice are better considered edible seeds, although some references list them as fruits. Edible gymnosperm seeds are often misleadingly given fruit names, e.g., pine nuts, ginkgo nuts, and juniper berries.

A fruit results from maturation of one or more flowers, and the gynoecium of the flower(s) forms all or part of the fruit.

Inside the ovary/ovaries are one or more ovules where the megagametophyte contains the mega gamete or egg cell. After double fertilization, these ovules will become seeds. The ovules are fertilized in a process that starts with pollination, which involves the movement of pollen from the stamens to the stigma of flowers. After pollination, a tube grows from the pollen through the stigma into the ovary to the ovule and two sperm are transferred from the pollen to the megagametophyte. Within the megagametophyte one of the two sperm unites with the egg, forming a zygote, and the second sperm enters the central cell forming the endosperm mother cell, which completes the double fertilization process. Later the zygote will give rise to the embryo of the seed, and the endosperm mother cell will give rise to endosperm, a nutritive tissue used by the embryo.

As the ovules develop into seeds, the ovary begins to ripen and the ovary wall, the *pericarp*, may become fleshy (as in berries or drupes), or form a hard outer covering (as in nuts). In some multiseeded fruits, the extent to which the flesh develops is proportional to the number of fertilized ovules. The pericarp is often differentiated into two or three distinct layers called the *exocarp* (outer layer, also called epicarp), *mesocarp* (middle layer), and *endocarp* (inner layer). In some fruits, especially simple fruits derived from an inferior ovary, other parts of the flower (such as the floral tube, including the petals, sepals, and stamens), fuse with the ovary and ripen with it. In other cases, the sepals, petals and/or stamens and style of the flower fall off. When such other floral parts are a significant part of the fruit, it is called an *accessory fruit*. Since other parts of the flower may contribute to the structure of the fruit, it is important to study flower structure to understand how a particular fruit forms.

Fruits are so diverse that it is difficult to devise a classification scheme that includes all known fruits. Many common terms for seeds and fruit are incorrectly applied, a fact that complicates understanding of the terminology. Seeds are ripened ovules; fruits are the ripened ovaries or carpels that contain the seeds. To these two basic definitions can be added the clarification that in botanical terminology, a nut is not a type of fruit and not another term for seed, on the contrary to common terminology.

There are three general modes of fruit development:

- Apocarpous fruits develop from a single flower having one or more separate carpels, and they are the simplest fruits.
- Syncarpous fruits develop from a single gynoecium having two or more carpels fused together.
- Multiple fruits form from many different flowers.

Plant scientists have grouped fruits into three main groups, simple fruits, aggregate fruits, and composite or multiple fruits. The groupings are not evolutionarily relevant, since many diverse plant taxa may be in the same group, but reflect how the flower organs are arranged and how the fruits develop.

Simple Fruit

Epigynous berries are simple fleshy fruit. From top right: cranberries, lingonberries, blueberries red huckleberries

Simple fruits can be either dry or fleshy, and result from the ripening of a simple or compound ovary in a flower with only one pistil. Dry fruits may be either dehiscent (opening to discharge seeds), or indehiscent (not opening to discharge seeds). Types of dry, simple fruits, with examples of each, are:

- Achene — Most commonly seen in aggregate fruits (e.g. strawberry)

- Capsule — (Brazil nut)
- Caryopsis — (Wheat)
- Cypsela — An achene-like fruit derived from the individual florets in a capitulum (e.g. dandelion).
- Fibrous drupe — (coconut, walnut)
- Follicle — is formed from a single carpel, and opens by one suture (e.g. milkweed). More commonly seen in aggregate fruits (e.g. magnolia)
- Legume — pea, bean, peanut)
- Loment — a type of indehiscent legume
- Nut — hazelnut, beech, oak acorn)
- Samara — (elm, ash, maplekey)
- Schizocarp — carrot seed)
- Silique — radish seed)
- Silicle — shepherd's purse)
- utricle — beet)

Lilium unripe capsule fruit

Fruits in which part or all of the *pericarp* (fruit wall) is fleshy at maturity are *simple fleshy fruits.* Types of fleshy, simple fruits (with examples) are:

- berry — redcurrant, gooseberry, tomato, cranberry)
- stone fruit or drupe plum, cherry, peach, apricot, olive)

Aggregate fruits form from single flowers that have multiple carpels which are not joined together, i.e. each pistil contains one carpel. Each pistil forms a fruitlet, and collectively the fruitlets are called an etaerio. Four types of aggregate fruits include etaerios of achenes, follicles, drupelets, and berries. Ranunculaceae species, including *Clematis* and *Ranunculus* have an etaerio of achenes, *Calotropis* has an etaerio of follicles, and *Rubus* species like raspberry, have an etaerio of drupelets. *Annona* have Etaerio of berries.

The raspberry, whose pistils are termed *drupelets* because each is like a small drupe attached to the receptacle. In some bramble fruits (such as blackberry) the receptacle is elongated and part of the ripe fruit, making the blackberry an *aggregate-accessory* fruit. The strawberry is also an aggregate-accessory fruit, only one in which the seeds are contained in achenes. In all these examples, the fruit develops from a single flower with numerous pistils.

Multiple Fruits

A multiple fruit is one formed from a cluster of flowers (called an *inflorescence*). Each flower produces a fruit, but these mature into a single mass. Examples are the pineapple, edible fig, mulberry, osage-orange, and breadfruit.

In some plants, such as this noni, flowers are produced regularly along the stem and it is possible to see together examples of flowering, fruit development, and fruit ripening.

In the photograph on the right, stages of flowering and fruit development in the noni or Indian mulberry (*Morinda citrifolia*) can be observed on a single branch. First an inflorescence of white flowers called a head is produced. After fertilization, each flower develops into a drupe, and as the drupes expand, they become *connate* (merge) into a *multiple fleshy fruit* called a *syncarpet*.

Fruit Chart

To summarize common types of fleshy fruit (examples follow in the table below):

Berry	— Simple fruit and seeds created from a single ovary
Pepo	— Berries where the skin is hardened, like cucurbits
Hesperidium	— Berries with a rind and a juicy interior, like most citrus fruit

Compound fruit, which includes:

- Dewberry flowers. Note the multiple pistils, each of which will produce a drupelet. Each flower will become a blackberry-like aggregate fruit.
- An aggregate fruit, or *etaerio*, develops from a single flower with numerous simple pistils.
- Magnolia and Peony, collection of follicles developing from one flower.
- Tuliptree, collection of samaras.
- Sweet gum, collection of capsules.
- Teasel, collection of cypsellas.

The pome fruits of the family Rosaceae, (including apples, pears, rosehips, and saskatoon berry) are a syncarpous fleshy fruit, a simple fruit, developing from a half-inferior ovary.

Schizocarp fruits form from a syncarpous ovary and do not really dehisce, but split into segments.

- Aggregate fruit — with seeds from different ovaries of a single flower.
- Multiple fruit — fruits of separate flowers, merged or packed closely together.
- Accessory fruit — where some or all of the edible part is not generated by the ovary.

Seedlessness is an important feature of some fruits of commerce. Commercial cultivars of bananas and pineapples are examples of seedless fruits. Some cultivars of citrus fruits (especially navel oranges), satsumas, mandarin oranges, table grapes, grapefruit, and watermelons are valued for their seedlessness. In some species, seedlessness is the result of *parthenocarpy*, where fruits set without fertilization. Parthenocarpic fruit set may or may not require pollination but most seedless citrus fruits require stimulus from pollination to produce fruit.

Seedless bananas and grapes are triploids, and seedlessness results from the abortion of the embryonic plant that is produced by fertilization, a phenomenon known as *stenospermocarpy* which requires normal pollination and fertilization.

Seed Dissemination

Variations in fruit structures largely depend on the mode of dispersal of the seeds they contain. This dispersal can be achieved by animals, wind, water, or explosive dehiscence.

Some fruits have coats covered with spikes or hooked burrs, either to prevent themselves from being eaten by animals or to stick to the hairs, feathers or legs of animals, using them as dispersal agents. Examples include cocklebur and unicorn plant.

The sweet flesh of many fruits is 'deliberately' appealing to animals, so that the seeds held within are eaten and 'unwittingly' carried away and deposited at a distance from the parent. Likewise, the nutritious, oily kernels of nuts are appealing to rodents (such as squirrels) who hoard them in the soil in order to avoid starving during the winter, thus giving those seeds that remain uneaten the chance to germinate and grow into a new plant away from their parent.

Other fruits are elongated and flattened out naturally and so become thin, like wings or helicopter blades, e.g. maple, tuliptree and elm. This is an evolutionary mechanism to increase dispersal distance away from the parent via wind. Other wind-dispersed fruit have tiny *parachutes*, e.g. dandelion and salsify.

Coconut fruits can float thousands of miles in the ocean to spread seeds. Some other fruits that can disperse via water are nipa palm and screw pine.

Some fruits fling seeds substantial distances (up to 100 m in sandbox tree) via explosive dehiscence or other mechanisms, e.g. impatiens and squirting cucumber.

Uses

Many hundreds of fruits, including fleshy fruits like apple, peach, pear, kiwifruit, watermelon and mango are commercially valuable as human food, eaten both fresh and as jams, marmalade and other preserves. Fruits are also in manufactured foods like cookies, muffins, yoghurt, ice cream, cakes, and many more. Many fruits are used to make beverages, such as fruit juices (orange juice, apple juice, grape juice, etc) or alcoholic beverages, such as wine or brandy. Apples are often used to make vinegar. Fruits are also used for gift giving, Fruit Basket and Fruit Bouquet are some common forms of fruit gifts.

Many vegetables are botanical fruits, including tomato, bell pepper, eggplant, okra, squash, pumpkin, green bean, cucumber and zucchini. Olive fruit is pressed for olive oil. Spices like vanilla, paprika, allspice and black pepper are derived from berries.

Nutritional Value

Fruits are generally high in fiber, water and vitamin C. Fruits also contain various phytochemicals that do not yet have an RDA/RDI listing under most nutritional factsheets, and which research indicates are required for proper long-term cellular health and disease prevention. Regular consumption of fruit is associated with reduced risks of cancer, cardiovascular disease, stroke, Alzheimer disease, cataracts, and some of the functional declines associated with aging.

Non-food Uses

Because fruits have been such a major part of the human diet, different cultures have developed many different uses for various fruits that they do not depend on as being edible. Many dry fruits are used as decorations or in dried flower arrangements, such as unicorn plant, lotus, wheat, annual honesty and milkweed. Ornamental trees and shrubs are often cultivated for their colourful fruits, including holly, pyracantha, viburnum, skimmia, beautyberry and cotoneaster.

Fruits of opium poppy are the source of opium which contains the drugs morphine and codeine, as well as the biologically inactive chemical theabaine from which the drug oxycodone is synthysized. Osage orange fruits are used to repel cockroaches Bayberry fruits provide a wax often used to make candles. Many fruits provide natural dyes, e.g. walnut, sumac, cherry and mulberry. Dried gourds are used as decorations, water jugs, bird houses, musical instruments, cups and dishes. Pumpkins are carved into Jack-o'-lanterns for Halloween. The spiny fruit of burdock or cocklebur were the inspiration for the invention of Velcro.

Coir is a fibre from the fruit of coconut that is used for doormats, brushes, mattresses, floortiles, sacking, insulation and as a growing medium for container plants. The shell of the coconut fruit is used to make souvenir heads, cups, bowls, musical instruments and bird houses.

Fruit is often used as a subject of still life paintings.

For food safety, the CDC recommends proper fruit handling and preparation to reduce the risk of food contamination and foodborne illness. Fresh fruits and vegetables should carefully be selected. At the store, they should not be damaged or bruised and pre-cut pieces should be refrigerated or surrounded by ice. All fruits and vegetables should be rinsed before eating. This recommendation also applies to produce with rinds or skins that are not eaten. It should be done just before preparing or eating to avoid premature spoilage. Fruits and vegetables should be kept separate from raw foods like meat, poultry, and seafood, as well as utensils that have come in contact with raw foods. Fruits and vegetables, if they are not going to be cooked, should be thrown away if they have touched raw meat, poultry, seafood or eggs. All cut, peeled, or cooked fruits and vegetables should be refrigerated within two hours. After a certain time, harmful bacteria may grow on them and increase the risk of foodborne illness.

Storage

The plant hormone ethylene causes ripening of many (but not all) types of fruit. Maintaining fruits in an efficient cold chain is optimal for post harvest storage. The aim is to extend and ensure shelf life. All fruits benefit from proper post harvest care.

14 Flowering Plant

The *flowering plants* or *angiosperms* (*Angiospermae* or *Magnoliophyta*) are the most diverse group of land plants. The flowering plants and the gymnosperms are the only extant groups of seed plants. The flowering plants are distinguished from other seed plants by a series of apomorphies, or derived characteristics.

The ancestors of flowering plants diverged from gymnosperms around 245-202 million years ago, and the first flowering plants known to exist are from 140 million years ago. They became widespread around 100 million years ago, but replaced conifers as the dominant trees only around 60-100 million years ago.

Angiosperm Derived Characteristics

Flowers

The flowers, which are the reproductive organs of flowering plants, are the most remarkable feature distinguishing them from other seed plants. Flowers aid angiosperms by enabling a wider range of adaptability and broadening the ecological niches open to them. This has allowed flowering plants to largely dominate terrestrial ecosystems.

Stamens with Two Pairs of Pollen Sacs

Stamens are much lighter than the corresponding organs of gymnosperms and have contributed to the diversification of angiosperms through time with adaptations to specialized pollination syndromes, such as particular pollinators. Stamens have also become modified through time to prevent self-fertilization, which has permitted further diversification, allowing angiosperms eventually to fill more niches.

Reduced Male Parts, Three Cells

The male gametophyte in angiosperms is significantly reduced in size compared to those of gymnosperm seed plants. The smaller pollen decreases the time from pollination — the pollen grain reaching the female plant — to fertilization of the ovary; in gymnosperms fertilization can occur up to a year after pollination, while in angiosperms the fertilization begins very soon after pollination. The shorter time leads to angiosperm plants setting seeds sooner and faster than gymnosperms, which is a distinct evolutionary advantage.

Closed carpel enclosing the ovules (carpel or carpels and accessory parts may become the fruit).

The closed carpel of angiosperms also allows adaptations to specialized pollination syndromes and controls. This helps to prevent self-fertilization, thereby maintaining increased diversity. Once the ovary is fertilized, the carpel and some surrounding tissues develop into a fruit. This fruit often serves as an attractant to seed-dispersing animals. The resulting cooperative relationship presents another advantage to angiosperms in the process of dispersal.

Reduced Female Gametophyte, Seven Cells with Eight Nuclei

The reduced female gametophyte, like the reduced male gametophyte, may be an adaptation allowing for more rapid seed set, eventually leading to such flowering plant adaptations as annual herbaceous life cycles, allowing the flowering plants to fill even more niches.

Endosperm

Endosperm formation generally begins after fertilization and before the first division of the zygote. Endosperm is a highly nutritive tissue that can provide food for the developing embryo, the cotyledons, and sometimes for the seedling when it first appears.

These distinguishing characteristics taken together have made the angiosperms the most diverse and numerous land plants and the most commercially important group to humans. The major exception to the dominance of terrestrial ecosystems by flowering plants is the coniferous forest.

Land plants have existed for about 425 million years Early land plants reproduced sexually with flagellated, swimming sperm, like the green algae from which they evolved. An adaptation to terrestrialization was the development of upright meiosporangia for dispersal by spores to new habitats. This feature is lacking in the descendants of their nearest algal relatives, the Charophycean green algae. A later terrestrial adaptation took place with retention of the delicate, a vascular sexual stage, the gametophyte, within the tissues of the vascular sporophyte. This occurred by spore germination within sporangia rather than spore release, as in non-seed plants. A current example of how this might have happened can be seen in the precocious spore germination in Sellaginella, the spike-moss. The result for the ancestors of angiosperms was enclosing them in a case, the seed. The first seed bearing plants, like the ginkgo, and conifers (such as pines and firs), did not produce flowers. Interestingly, the pollen grains (males) of Ginkgo and cycads produce a pair of flagellated, mobile sperm cells that 'swim' down the developing pollen tube to the female and her eggs.

The apparently sudden appearance of relatively modern flowers in the fossil record posed such a problem for the theory of evolution that it was called an 'abominable mystery' by Charles Darwin. However, the fossil record has grown since the time of Darwin, and recently discovered angiosperm fossils such as *Archaefructus*, along with further discoveries of fossil gymnosperms, suggest how angiosperm characteristics may have been acquired in a series of steps. Several groups of extinct gymnosperms, particularly seed ferns, have been proposed as the ancestors of flowering plants but there is no continuous fossil evidence showing exactly how flowers evolved. Some older fossils, such as the upper Triassic *Sanmiguelia*, have been suggested. Based on current evidence, some propose that the ancestors of the angiosperms diverged from an unknown group of gymnosperms during the late Triassic (245-202 million years ago). A close relationship between angiosperms and gnetophytes, proposed on the basis of morphological evidence, has more recently been disputed on the basis of molecular evidence that suggest gnetophytes are instead more closely related to other gymnosperms.

The earliest known angiosperm macrofossil, *Archaefructus liaoningensis*, is dated to about 125 million years BP (the Cretaceous period), while pollen considered to be of angiosperm origin takes the fossil record back to about 130 million years BP. There is, however, circumstantial chemical evidence for the existence of angiosperms as early as 250 million years ago. Oleanane, a secondary metabolite produced by many flowering plants, has been found in Permian deposits of that age together with fossils of gigantopterids Gigantopterids are a group of extinct seed plants that share many morphological traits with flowering plants, although they are not known to have been flowering plants themselves.

Recent DNA analysis (molecular systematics) show that *Amborella trichopoda*, found on the Pacific island of New

Caledonia, belongs to a sister group of the other flowering plants, and morphological studies suggest that it has features that may have been characteristic of the earliest flowering plants.

The great angiosperm radiation, when a great diversity of angiosperms appears in the fossil record, occurred in the mid-Cretaceous (approximately 100 million years ago). However, a study in 2007 estimated that the division of the five most recent (the genus *Ceratophyllum*, the family Chloranthaceae, the eudicots, the magnoliids, and the monocots) of the eight main groups occurred around 140 million years ago. By the late Cretaceous, angiosperms appear to have dominated environments formerly occupied by ferns and cycadophytes, but large canopy-forming trees replaced conifers as the dominant trees only close to the end of the Cretaceous 65 millions years ago or even later, at the beginning of the Tertiary. The radiation of herbaceous angiosperm occurred much later. Yet, many fossil plants recognizable as belonging to modern families (including beech, oak, maple, and magnolia) appeared already at late Cretaceous.

It is generally assumed that the function of flowers, from the start, was to involve mobile animals in their reproduction processes. That is, pollen can be scattered even if the flower is not brightly colored or oddly shaped in a way that attracts animals; however, by expending the energy required to create such traits, angiosperms can enlist the aid of animals and thus reproduce more efficiently.

Island genetics provides one proposed explanation for the sudden, fully developed appearance of flowering plants. Island genetics is believed to be a common source of speciation in general, especially when it comes to radical adaptations that seem to have required inferior transitional forms. Flowering plants may have evolved in an isolated setting like an island or island chain, where the plants bearing them were able to develop a highly specialized relationship with some specific animal (a wasp, for example). Such a relationship, with a hypothetical wasp carrying pollen from one plant to another much the way fig wasps do today, could result in both the plant(s) and their partners developing a high degree of specialization. Note that the wasp example is not incidental; bees, which apparently evolved specifically due to mutualistic plant relationships, are descended from wasps.

Animals are also involved in the distribution of seeds. Fruit, which is formed by the enlargement of flower parts, is frequently a seed-dispersal tool that attracts animals to eat or otherwise disturb it, incidentally scattering the seeds it contains. While many such mutualistic relationships remain too fragile to survive competition and spread widely, flowering proved to be an unusually effective means of reproduction, spreading (whatever its origin) to become the dominant form of land plant life.

Flower ontogeny uses a combination of genes normally responsible for forming new shoots The most primitive flowers are thought to have had a variable number of flower parts, often separate from (but in contact with) each other. The flowers would have tended to grow in a spiral pattern, to be bisexual (in plants, this means both male and female parts on the same flower), and to be dominated by the ovary (female part). As flowers grew more advanced, some variations developed parts fused together, with a much more specific number and design, and with either specific sexes per flower or plant, or at least 'ovary inferior'.

Flower evolution continues to the present day; modern flowers have been so profoundly influenced by humans that some of them cannot be pollinated in nature. Many modern, domesticated flowers used to be simple weeds, which only sprouted when the ground was disturbed. Some of them tended to grow with human crops, perhaps already having symbiotic companion plant relationships with them, and the prettiest did not get plucked because of their beauty, developing a dependence upon and special adaptation to human affection.

The botanical term 'Angiosperm', from the Ancient Greek, *angeíon* (receptacle, vessel) and, (seed), was coined in the form Angiospermae by Paul Hermann in 1690, as the name of that one of his primary divisions of the plant kingdom. This included flowering plants possessing seeds enclosed in capsules, distinguished from his Gymnospermae, or flowering plants with achenial or schizo-carpic fruits, the whole fruit or each of its pieces being here regarded as a seed and naked. The term and its antonym were maintained by Carolus Linnaeus with the same sense, but with restricted application, in the names of the orders of his class Didynamia. Its use with any approach to its modern scope only became possible after 1827, when Robert Brown established the existence of truly naked ovules in the Cycadeae and Coniferae, and applied to them the name Gymnosperms. From that time onwards, so long as these Gymnosperms were, as was usual, reckoned as dicotyledonous flowering plants, the term Angiosperm was used antithetically by botanical writers, with varying scope, as a group-name for other dicotyledonous plants.

In 1851, Hofmeister discovered the changes occurring in the embryo-sac of flowering plants, and determined the correct relationships of these to the Cryptogamia. This fixed the position of Gymnosperms as a class distinct from Dicotyledons, and the term Angiosperm then gradually came to be accepted as the suitable designation for the whole of the flowering plants other than Gymnosperms, including the classes of Dicotyledons and Monocotyledons. This is the sense in which the term is used today.

In most taxonomies, the flowering plants are treated as a coherent group. The most popular descriptive name has been Angiospermae (Angiosperms), with Anthophyta ('flowering plants') a second choice. These names are not linked to any rank. The Wettstein system and the Engler system use the name Angiospermae, at the assigned rank of subdivision. The Reveal system treated flowering plants as subdivision Magnoliophytina, but later split it to Magnoliopsida, Liliopsida and Rosopsida. The Takhtajan system and Cronquist system treat this group at the rank of division, leading to the name Magnoliophyta (from the family name Magnoliaceae). The Dahlgren system and Thorne system (1992) treat this group at the rank of class, leading to the name Magnoliopsida. However, the APG system, of 1998, and the APG II system, of 2003 , do not treat it as a formal taxon but rather treat it as a clade without a formal botanical name and use the name angiosperms for this clade.

The internal classification of this group has undergone considerable revision. The Cronquist system, proposed by Arthur Cronquist in 1968 and published in its full form in 1981, is still widely used, but is no longer believed to accurately reflect phylogeny. A general consensus about how the flowering plants should be arranged has recently begun to emerge, through the work of the Angiosperm Phylogeny Group, who published an influential reclassification of the angiosperms in 1998. An update incorporating more recent research was published as APG II in 2003.

Recent studies, as by the APG, show that the monocots form holophyletic or monophyletic group; this clade is given the name *monocots*. However, the dicots are not (they are a paraphyletic group). Nevertheless, within the dicots a monophyletic group does exist, called the *eudicots* or *tricolpates*, and including most of the dicots. The name *tricolpates* derives from a type of pollen found widely within this group. The name *eudicots* is formed combining *dicot* with the prefix *eu-* (from Greek, for 'well', or 'good', botanically indicating 'true'), as the eudicots share the characters traditionally attributed to the dicots, such as flowers with four or five parts (four or five petals, four or five sepals). Separating this group of eudicots from the rest of the (former) dicots leaves a remainder, which sometimes are called informally *palaeodicots* (Greek prefix *'palaeo-'* means 'old'). As this remnant group is not monophyletic this is a term of convenience only.

Flowering Plant Diversity

The number of species of flowering plants is estimated to be in the range of 250,000 to 400,000. The number of families in APG (1998) was 462. In APG II (2003) it is not settled; at maximum it is 457, but within this number there are 55 optional segregates, so that the minimum number of families in this system is 402.

The diversity of flowering plants is not evenly distributed. Nearly all species belong to the eudicot (75%), monocot (23%) and magnoliid (2%) clades. The remaining 5 clades contain a little over 250 species in total, i.e., less than 0.1 per cent of flowering plant diversity, divided among 9 families.

The amount and complexity of tissue-formation in flowering plants exceeds that of Gymnosperms. The vascular bundles of the stem are arranged such that the xylem and phloem form concentric rings.

In the Dicotyledons, the bundles in the very young stem are arranged in an open ring, separating a central pith from an outer cortex. In each bundle, separating the xylem and phloem, is a layer of meristem or active formative tissue known as cambium. By the formation of a layer of cambium between the bundles (interfascicular cambium) a complete ring is formed, and a regular periodical increase in thickness results from the development of xylem on the inside and phloem on the outside. The soft phloem becomes crushed, but the hard wood persists and forms the bulk of the stem and branches of the woody perennial. Owing to differences in the character of the elements produced at the beginning and end of the season, the wood is marked out in transverse section into concentric rings, one for each season of growth, called annual rings.

Among the Monocotyledons, the bundles are more numerous in the young stem and are scattered through the ground tissue. They contain no cambium and once formed the stem increases in diameter only in exceptional cases.

Traditionally, the flowering plants are divided into two groups, which in the Cronquist system are called *Magnoliopsida* (at the rank of class, formed from the family name *Magnoliacae*) and *Liliopsida* (at the rank of class, formed from the family name *Liliaceae*). Other descriptive names allowed by Article 16 of the ICBN include *Dicotyledones* or *Dicotyledoneae*, and *Monocotyledones* or *Monocotyledoneae*, which have a long history of use. In English a member of either group may be called a *dicotyledon* (plural *dicotyledons*) and *monocotyledon* (plural *monocotyledons*), or abbreviated, as *dicot* (plural *dicots*) and *monocot* (plural *monocots*). These names derive from the observation that the dicots most often have two *cotyledons*, or embryonic leaves, within each seed. The monocots usually have only one, but the rule is not absolute either way. From a diagnostic point of view the number of cotyledons is neither a particularly handy nor reliable character.

The characteristic feature of angiosperms is the flower. Flowers show remarkable variation in form and elaboration, and provide the most trustworthy external characteristics for establishing relationships among angiosperm species. The function of the flower is to ensure fertilization of the ovule and development of fruit containing seeds. The floral apparatus may arise terminally on a shoot or from the axil of a leaf (where the petiole attaches to the stem). Occasionally, as in violets, a flower arises singly in the axil of an ordinary foliage-leaf. More typically, the flower-bearing portion of the plant is sharply distinguished from the foliage-bearing or vegetative portion, and forms a more or less elaborate branch-system called an inflorescence.

The reproductive cells produced by flowers are of two kinds. Microspores, which will divide to become pollen grains, are the 'male' cells and are borne in the stamens (or microsporophylls). The 'female' cells called megaspores, which will divide to become the egg-cell (megagametogenesis), are contained in the ovule and enclosed in the carpel (or megasporophyll).

The flower may consist only of these parts, as in willow, where each flower comprises only a few stamens or two carpels. Usually other structures are present and serve to protect the sporophylls and to form an envelope attractive to pollinators. The individual members of these surrounding structures are known as sepals and petals (or tepals in flowers such as *Magnolia* where sepals and petals are not distinguishable from each other). The outer series (calyx of sepals) is usually green and leaf-like, and functions to protect the rest of the flower, especially the bud. The inner series (corolla of petals) is generally white or brightly coloured, and is more delicate in structure. It functions to attract insect or bird pollinators. Attraction is effected by colour, scent, and nectar, which may be secreted in some part of the flower. The characteristics that attract pollinators account for the popularity of flowers and flowering plants among humans.

While the majority of flowers are perfect or hermaphrodite (having both male and female parts in the same flower structure), flowering plants have developed numerous morphological and physiological mechanisms to reduce or prevent self-fertilization. Heteromorphic flowers have short carpels and long stamens, or vice versa, so animal pollinators cannot easily transfer pollen to the pistil (receptive part of the carpel). Homomorphic flowers may employ a biochemical (physiological) mechanism called self-incompatibility to discriminate between self-and non-self pollen grains. In other species, the male and female parts are morphologically separated, developing on different flowers.

Double fertilization refers to a process in which two sperm cells fertilize cells in the ovary. This process begins when a pollen grain adheres to the stigma of the pistil (female reproductive structure), germinates, and grows a long pollen tube. While this pollen tube is growing, a haploid generative cell travels down the tube behind the tube nucleus. The generative cell divides by mitosis to produce two haploid (n) sperm cells. As the pollen tube grows, it makes its way from the stigma, down the style and into the ovary. Here the pollen tube reaches the micropyle of the ovule and digests its way into one of the synergids, releasing its contents (which include the sperm cells). The synergid that the cells were released into degenerates and one sperm makes its way to fertilize the egg cell, producing a diploid ($2n$) zygote. The second sperm cell fuses with both central cell nuclei, producing a triploid ($3n$) cell. As the zygote develops into an embryo, the triploid cell develops into the endosperm, which serves as the embryo's food supply. The ovary now will develop into fruit and the ovule will develop into seed.

Fruit and Seed

As the development of embryo and endosperm proceeds within the embryo-sac, the sac wall enlarges and combines with the nucellus (which is likewise enlarging) and the integument to form the *seed-coat.* The ovary wall develops to form the fruit or pericarp, whose form is closely associated with the manner of distribution of the seed.

The character of the seed-coat bears a definite relation to that of the fruit. They protect the embryo and aid in dissemination; they may also directly promote germination. Among plants with indehiscent fruits, the fruit generally provides protection for the embryo and secures dissemination. In this case, the seed-coat is only slightly developed. If the fruit is dehiscent and the seed is exposed, the seed-coat is generally well developed, and must discharge the functions otherwise executed by the fruit.

Agriculture is almost entirely dependent on angiosperms, either directly or indirectly through livestock feed. Of all the families plants, the Poaceae, or grass family, is by far the most important, providing the bulk of all feedstocks (rice, corn – maize, wheat, barley, rye, oats, pearl millet, sugar cane, sorghum). The Fabaceae, or legume family, comes in second place. Also of high importance are the Solanaceae, or nightshade family (potatoes, tomatoes, and peppers, among others), the Cucurbitaceae, or gourd family (also including pumpkins and melons), the Brassicaceae, or mustard plant family (including rapeseed and cabbage), and the Apiaceae, or parsley family. Many of our fruits come from the Rutaceae, or rue family, and the Rosaceae, or rose family (including apples, pears, cherries, apricots, plums, etc.).

In some parts of the world, certain single species assume paramount importance because of their variety of uses, for example the coconut (*Cocos nucifera*) on Pacific atolls, and the olive (*Olea europaea*) in the Mediterranean region.

Flowering plants also provide economic resources in the form of wood, paper, fiber (cotton, flax, and hemp, among others), medicines (digitalis, camphor), decorative and landscaping plants, and many other uses. The main area in which they are surpassed by other plants is timber production.

Floristry

Floristry is the general term used to describe the professional floral trade. It encompasses flower care and handling, floral design or flower arranging, merchandising, and display and flower delivery. Wholesale florists sell bulk flowers and related supplies to professionals in the trade. Retail florists offer fresh flowers and related products and services to consumers.

Floristry is a term that refers to the cultivation of flowers as well as their arrangement, and to the business of selling them. However, the floral industry is the basic drive behind floristry. Florist shops, along with online stores are the main flower-only outlets, but supermarkets, garden supply stores and filling stations also sell flowers.

Floral Design or floral arts is the art of creating flower arrangements in vases, bowls, baskets or other containers, or making bouquets and compositions from cut flowers, foliages, herbs, ornamental grasses and other botanical materials. Often the terms 'floral design' and 'floristry' are considered synonymous. Florists are people who work with flowers and plants, generally at the retail level. The term is not to be confused with floristics (the study of distribution and relationships of plant species over geographic areas.). Floristry is also not to be confused with horticulture which more broadly relates to the cultivation of flowers and plants.

The craft of floristry, or being a florist, involves various skills and creativity. A florist should be able to select flowers and other floral supplies and materials that will look good together (based on principles and elements of floral design or market demands), know how to handle and arrange flowers and plants so they will remain fresh as long as possible, and would be desirable for purchase, which also involves knowledge of customers' requirements and expectations. Ability to create a variety of floral designs such as wreaths, bouquets, corsages, boutonnières/'buttonholes', permanent arrangements and other more complicated arrangements is also important.

The flowers sold in florist shops typically represent the varieties abundantly available in the season but also include blossoms flown in from around the world. Basic varieties include roses, tulips, irises, orchids and lilies. Fashion sometimes plays a role in floristry; what is considered the flower that everyone needs to have today can change very quickly.

Some shops also stock gift baskets, fruits, and chocolates as well as flowers, whereas some shops will purchase these things only when needed for an order. Floral business is seasonal and is heavily influenced by the following holidays and events: Christmas, Valentine's Day, Administrative Professionals' Day, Mothers' Day, All Souls Day, Advent, Easter, weddings and funerals. These occasions make up the largest part of the business, with the sale of house plants and home decor being a smaller, but more constant, part. Flowers for personal enjoyment as well as those selected to celebrate birthdays, anniversaries, thank-you's and get well wishes are also a significant portion of a florist's business.

Floral education, both formal and informal, is another significant segment of the floral industry. Established Floral Designers and Artists impart their craft to students interested in floral design as hobby or career. Courses are generally available in university Horticulture departments, through community colleges, via private post-secondary vocational schools and through professional florist trade associations.

The floral business has been impacted significantly by the corporate and social event world in as much as flowers play a large part in the decor of special events and meetings. Centerpieces, entryways, reception tables, bridal bouquets, wedding chuppahs and stage sets and only a few examples of how flowers are used in the business and social event arenas.

Styles of Floristry

Many nations have their own style of floral arranging.

Ikebana

Ikebana is a style of floral design that originated in Japan. Most well known for its simplicity of line and form, Ikebana is a design style primarily practiced for personal enjoyment.

English Garden

English Garden style is traditionally an English form of floral design. Stems are placed in a radial fashion and feature abundant use of seasonal flowers and foliages. These designs are often done as low, tufted mounds, or taller vase arrangements that are all-sided (360°), and incorporate garden flowers like roses, delphinium and peonies. Many florists that follow this design style do not use Baby's Breath, Carnations and Leatherleaf.

High Style

High Style is a catch-all term to describe contemporary, linear designs that highlights unique forms of both individual floral materials and of the designs themselves. Arrangements generally feature negative space and incorporate asymmetric placement of materials. The style stands in direct contrast to traditional radial arrangements such as English Garden.

High Style designs often incorporate unique, exotic or tropical flowers such as such as Bird of Paradise, Anthurium and Protea but may also employ more common blossoms.

Fresh Flowers Sources

There are three major sources of fresh flowers for retail florists in North America: local growers, local wholesalers and flower auctions.

Miami is considered to be the main distribution point for imported fresh flowers. Many local wholesalers are purchasing fresh flower stock from importers in Miami to resale to local florist in their areas. Wholesale flower districts present in many North American cities such as New York, Boston and San Francisco. Flower auctions are run using Dutch clock system and mainly located in Canada: Toronto, Montreal, and Vancouver. Internationally there are hundreds of wholesale flower markets and auctions, the largest of which is located in Aalsmeer, Holland, the Bloemenveiling Aalsmeer. Other major markets include the fledgling Dubai Flower Centre and the Ota Flower Market in Tokyo, Japan.

Shop Layout

Generally, a florist's shop will contain a large array of flowers, sometimes displayed on the street, or will have a large plate glass window to display the flowers. To keep them fresh, the flowers will be inside of a cooler and kept in water, generally in glass or plastic vases or other containers. Most shops have a cooler near the front of the store with large glass doors so that customers can easily view the contents. Some shops also have another cooler out of the customers' view where they keep extra stock and arrangements for customers' orders. Most stores have a back section in which the designers can work on orders with more privacy.

Significance of Particular Flowers

Typically, a florist will organize flowers by season and holiday. Flowers have various different meanings in different cultures. The holidays and events for which flowers are used vary. Poppies are used to remember fallen soldiers only in Great Britain and the Commonwealth countries. The cultural meaning of colours also strongly affects the choice and use of flowers. People often prefer flowers that are associated with their ethnic group or country, and various colours may have special meanings of luck or death or love or other basic human traits. To some, a flower such as a red rose might mean love, but to others it might be considered indecent or simply puzzling.

The vastly divergent views on the colour white can also lead to major flower issues. While white represents death in many Asian cultures, it is simultaneously a symbol of purity and innocence in many European and American cultures. Such differences can lead to difficult issues when a bouquet of white lilies, for example, is delivered.

Supermarket Flowers

Cut flowers are widely sold in supermarkets and gas stations. These outlets offer a limited selection, usually in the form of mixed bouquets and roses by the dozen. Flowers purchased at these outlets are generally less expensive than the same flowers purchased at a florist shop.

Internet Sales

The World Wide Web has had a significant impact on traditional florists, with the North American market experiencing a more than 20 per cent decline in traditional, independently owned flower shops since 1998. Purchases from shops are slowly being overtaken by online flower delivery ordering and floral wire services. However, some independent florists have taken to having their own online store, where customers can order online as well as on the telephone.

Evolution of Plants

The *evolution of plants* occurred through increasing levels of complexity, from the earliest algal mats, through bryophytes, lycopods, ferns and gymnosperms to the complex angiosperms of today. While the simple plants continue to thrive, especially in the environments in which they evolved, each new grade of organisation has eventually become more 'successful' than its predecessors by most measures. Further, most cladistic analyses, where they agree, suggest that each 'more complex' group arose from the most complex group at the time.

Evidence suggests that an algal scum formed on the land 1,200 million years ago, but it was not until the Ordovician period, around 450 million years ago, that land plants appeared. These began to diversify in the late Silurian period, around 420 million years ago, and the fruits of their diversification are displayed in remarkable detail in an early Devonian fossil assemblage known as the Rhynie chert. This chert preserved early plants in cellular detail, petrified in volcanic springs. By the middle of the Devonian period most of the features recognised in plants today are present, including roots, leaves and seeds. By the late Devonian, plants had reached a degree of sophistication that allowed them to form forests of tall trees. Evolutionary innovation continued after the Devonian period. Most plant groups were relatively unscathed by the Permo-Triassic extinction event, although the structures of communities changed. This may have set the scene for the evolution of flowering plants in the Triassic (~200 million years ago), which exploded in the Cretaceous and Tertiary. The latest major group of plants to evolve were the grasses, which became important in the mid Tertiary, from around 40 million years ago. The grasses, as well as many other groups, evolved new mechanisms of metabolism to survive the low CO_2 and warm, dry conditions of the tropics over the last 10 million years.

Land plants evolved from chlorophyte algae, perhaps as early as 510 million years ago; their closest living relatives are the charophytes, specifically Charales. Assuming that the Charales' habit has changed little since the divergence of lineages, this means that the land plants evolved from a branched, filamentous, haplontic alga, dwelling in shallow, fresh water, perhaps at the edge of desiccating pools. Co-operative interactions with fungi may have helped early plants adapt to the stresses of the terrestrial realm.

Plants were not the first photosynthesisers on land, though: consideration of weathering rates suggests that organisms were already living on the land 1,200 million years ago, and microbial fossils have been found in freshwater lake deposits from 1,000 million years ago, but the carbon isotope record suggests that they were too scarce to impact the atmospheric composition until around 850 million years ago. These organisms were probably small and simple, forming little more than an 'algal scum'.

The first evidence of plants on land comes from spore tetrads attributed to land plants from the Mid-Ordovician. (early Llanvirn, ~470 million years ago), The microstructure of the earliest spores resembles that of modern liverwort spores, suggesting they share an equivalent grade of organisation. It could be that atmospheric 'poisoning' prevented eukaryotes from colonising the land prior to this, or it could simply have taken a great time for the necessary complexity to evolve.

Trilete spores appear soon afterwards, in the Late Ordovician. Trilete spores are the progeny of spore tetrads that consist of four identical, connected spores, produced when a single cell undergoes meiosis. Spore tetrads are borne by all land plants, and some algae. Depending exactly when the tetrad splits, each of the four spores may bear a 'trilete mark', a *Y*-shape, reflecting the points at which each cell was squashed up against its neighbours. However, in order for this to happen, the spore walls must be sturdy and resistant at an early stage. This resistance is closely associated with having a desiccation-resistant outer wall — a trait only of use when spores have to survive out of water. Indeed, even those embryophytes that have returned to the water lack a resistant wall, thus don't bear trilete marks. A close examination of algal spores shows that none have trilete spores, either because their walls are not resistant enough, or in those rare cases where it is, the spores disperse before they are squashed enough to develop the mark, or don't fit into a tetrahedral tetrad.

The earliest megafossils of land plants were thalloid organisms, which dwelt in fluvial wetlands and are found to have covered most of an early Silurian flood plain. They could only survive when the land was waterlogged.

Once plants had reached the land, there were two approaches to desiccation. The bryophytes avoid it or give in to it, restricting their ranges to moist settings, or drying out and putting their metabolism 'on hold' until more water arrives. Tracheophytes resist desiccation. They all bear a waterproof outer cuticle layer wherever they are exposed to air (as do some bryophytes), to reduce water loss — but since a total covering would cut them off from CO_2 in the atmosphere, they rapidly evolved stomata — small openings to allow gas exchange. Tracheophytes also developed vascular tissue to aid in the movement of water within the organisms, and moved away from a gametophyte dominated life cycle.

The establishment of a land-based flora permitted the accumulation of oxygen in the atmosphere as never before, as the new hordes of land plants pumped it out as a waste product. When this concentration rose above 13 per cent, it permitted the possibility of wildfire. This is first recorded in the early Silurian fossil record by charcoalified plant fossils. Apart from a controversial gap in the Late Devonian, charcoal is present ever since.

Charcoalification is an important taphonomic mode. Wildfire drives off the volatile compounds, leaving only a shell of pure carbon. This is not a viable food source for herbivores or detritovores, so is prone to preservation; it is also robust, so can withstand pressure and display exquisite, sometimes sub-cellular, detail.

Changing Life Cycles

All multicellular plants have a life cycle comprising two phases (often confusingly referred to as 'generations'). One is termed the gametophyte, has a single set of chromosomes (denoted 1n), and produces gametes (sperm and eggs). The other is termed the sporophyte, has paired chromosomes (denoted 2n), and produces spores. The two phases may be identical, or phenomenally different.

The overwhelming pattern in plant evolution is for a reduction of the gametophytic phase, and the increase in sporophyte dominance. The algal ancestors to land plants were almost certainly haplobiontic, being haploid for all their life cycles, with a unicellular zygote providing the 2n stage. All land plants (i.e. embryophytes) are diplobiontic — that is, both the haploid and diploid stages are multicellular.

There are two competing theories to explain the appearance of a diplobiontic lifecycle.

1. The ***interpolation theory*** (also known as the *antithetic* or *intercalary theory*) holds that the sporophyte phase was a fundamentally new invention, caused by the mitotic division of a freshly germinated zygote, continuing until meiosis produces spores. This theory implies that the first sporophytes would bear a very different morphology to the gametophyte, on which they would have been dependent. This seems to fit well with what we know of the bryophytes, in which a vegetative thalloid gametophyte is parasitised by simple sporophytes, which often comprise no more than a sporangium on a stalk. Increasing complexity of the ancestrally simple sporophyte, including the eventual acquisition of photosynthetic cells, would free it from its dependence on a gametophyte, as we see in some hornworts (*Anthoceros*), and eventually result in the sporophyte developing organs and vascular tissue, and becoming the dominant phase, as in the tracheophytes (vascular plants). This theory may be supported by observations that smaller *Cooksonia* individuals must have been supported by a gametophyte generation. The observed appearance of larger axial sizes, with room for photosynthetic tissue and thus self-sustainability, provides a possible route for the development of a self-sufficient sporophyte phase.
2. The alternative hypothesis is termed the ***transformation theory*** (or *homologous theory*). This posits that the sporophyte appeared suddenly by a delay in the occurrence of meiosis after the zygote germinated. Since the same genetic material would be employed, the haploid and diploid phases would look the same. This explains the behaviour of some algae, which produce alternating phases of identical sporophytes and gametophytes. Subsequent adaption to the desiccating land environment, which makes sexual reproduction difficult, would result in the

simplification of the sexually active gametophyte. and elaboration of the sporophyte phase to better disperse the waterproof spores. The tissue of sporophytes and gametophytes preserved in the Rhynie chert is of similar complexity, which is taken to support this hypothesis.

Water Transport

In order to photosynthesise, plants must uptake CO_2 from the atmosphere. However, this comes at a price: while stomata are open to allow CO_2 to enter, water can evaporate Water is lost much faster than CO_2 is absorbed, so plants need to replace it, and have developed systems to transport water from the moist soil to the site of photosynthesis. Early plants sucked water between the walls of their cells, then evolved the ability to control water loss (and CO_2 acquisition) through the use of stomata. Specialised water transport tissues soon evolved in the form of hydroids, tracheids, then secondary xylem, followed by an endodermis and ultimately vessels.

The high CO_2 levels of the Silu-Devonian, when early plants were colonising land, meant that the need for water was relatively low in the early days. As CO_2 was withdrawn from the atmosphere by plants, more water was lost in its capture, and more elegant transport mechanisms evolved. As water transport mechanisms, and waterproof cuticles, evolved, plants could survive without being continually covered by a film of water. This transition from poikilohydry to homoiohydry opened up new potential for colonisation. Plants were then faced with a balance, between transporting water as efficiently as possible and preventing transporting vessels to implode and cavitate.

During the Silurian, CO_2 was readily available, so little water needed expending to acquire it. By the end of the Carboniferous, when CO_2 levels had lowered to something approaching today's, around 17 times more water was lost per unit of CO_2 uptake. However, even in these 'easy' early days, water was at a premium, and had to be transported to parts of the plant from the wet soil to avoid desiccation. This early water transport took advantage of the cohesion-tension mechanism inherent in water. Water has a tendency to diffuse to areas that are drier, and this process is exacberated when water can be wicked along a fabric with small spaces. In small passages, such as that between the plant cell walls (or in tracheids), a column of water behaves like rubber — when molecules evaporate from one end, they literally pull the molecules behind them along the channels. Therefore transpiration alone provided the driving force for water transport in early plants. However, without dedicated transport vessels, the cohesion-tension mechanism cannot transport water more than about 2 cm, severely limiting the size of the earliest plants. This process demands a steady supply of water from one end, to maintain the chains; to avoid exhausing it, plants developed a waterproof cuticle. Early cuticle may not have had pores but did not cover the entire plant surface, so that gas exchange could continue. However, dehydration at times was inevitable; early plants cope with this by having a lot of water stored between their cell walls, and when it comes to it sticking out the tough times by putting life 'on hold' until more water is supplied.

In order to be free from the constraints of small size and constant moisture that the parenchymatic transport system inflicted, plants needed a more efficient water transport system. During the early Silurian, they developed specialized cells, which were lignified (or bore similar chemical compounds) to avoid implosion; this process coincided with cell death, allowing their innards to be emptied and water to be passed through them. These wider, dead, empty cells were a million times more conductive than the inter-cell method, giving the potential for transport over longer distances, and higher CO_2 diffusion rates.

The first macrofossils to bear water-transport tubes *in situ* are the early Devonian pretracheophytes *Aglaophyton* and *Horneophyton*, which have structures very similar to the hydroids of modern mosses. Plants continued to innovate new ways of reducing the resistance to flow within their cells, thereby increasing the efficiency of their water transport. Bands on the walls of tubes, in fact apparent from the early Silurian onwards, are an early improvisation to aid the easy flow of water. Banded tubes, as well as tubes with pitted ornamentation on their walls, were lignified and, when they form single celled conduits, are considered to be tracheids. These, the 'next generation' of transport cell design, have a more rigid structure than hydroids, allowing them to cope with higher levels of water pressure. Tracheids may have a single evolutionary origin, possibly within the hornworts, uniting all tracheophytes (but they may have evolved more than once).

Water transport requires regulation, and dynamic control is provided by stomata. By adjusting the amount of gas exchange, they can restrict the amount of water lost through transpiration. This is an important role where water supply is not constant, and indeed stomata appear to have evolved before tracheids, being present in the non-vascular hornworts.

An endodermis probably evolved during the Silu-Devonian, but the first fossil evidence for such a structure is Carboniferous. This structure in the roots covers the water transport tissue and regulates ion exchange (and prevents unwanted pathogens etc. from entering the water transport system). The endodermis can also provide an upwards pressure, forcing water out of the roots when transpiration is not enough of a driver.

Once plants had evolved this level of controlled water transport, they were truly homoiohydric, able to extract water from their environment through root-like organs rather than relying on a film of surface moisture, enabling them to grow to much greater size. As a result of their independence from their surroundings, they lost their ability to survive desiccation — a costly trait to retain.

During the Devonian, maximum xylem diameter increased with time, with the minimum diameter remaining pretty constant. By the middle Devonian, the tracheid diameter of some plant lineages had plateaued. Wider tracheids allow water to be transported faster, but the overall transport rate depends also on the overall cross-sectional area of the xylem bundle itself. The increase in vascular bundle thickness further seems to correlate with the width of plant axes, and plant height; it is also closely related to the appearance of leaves and increased stomatal density, both of which would increase the demand for water.

While wider tracheids with robust walls make it possible to achieve higher water transport pressures, this increases the problem of cavitation. Cavitation occurs when a bubble of air forms within a vessel, breaking the bonds between chains of water molecules and preventing them from pulling more water up with their cohesive tension. A tracheid, once cavitated, cannot have its embolism removed and return to service (except in a few advanced angiosperms which have developed a mechanism of doing so). Therefore it is well worth plants' while to avoid cavitation occurring. For this reason, pits in tracheid walls have very small diametres, to prevent air entering and allowing bubbles to nucleate. Freeze-thaw cycles are a major cause of cavitation Damage to a tracheid's wall almost inevitably leads to air leaking in and cavitation, hence the importance of many tracheids working in parallel.

Cavitation is hard to avoid, but once it has occurred plants have a range of mechanisms to contain the damage. Small pits link adjacent conduits to allow fluid to flow between them, but not air — although ironically these pits, which prevent the spread of embolisms, are also a major cause of them. These pitted surfaces further reduce the flow of water through the xylem by as much as 30 per cent. Conifers, by the Jurassic, developed an ingenious improvement, using valve-like structures to isolate cavitated elements. These torus-margo structures have a blob floating in the middle of a donut; when one side depressurises the blob is sucked into the torus and blocks further flow. Other plants simply accept cavitation; for instance, oaks grow a ring of wide vessels at the start of each spring, none of which survive the winter frosts. Maples use root pressure each spring to force sap upwards from the roots, squeezing out any air bubbles.

Growing to height also employed another trait of tracheids — the support offered by their lignified walls. Defunct tracheids were retained to form a strong, woody stem, produced in most instances by a secondary xylem. However, in early plants, tracheids were too mechanically vulnerable, and retained a central position, with a layer of tough sclerenchyma on the outer rim of the stems. Even when tracheids do take a structural role, they are supported by sclerenchymatic tissue.

Tracheids end with walls, which impose a great deal of resistance on flow; vessel members have perforated end walls, and are arranged in series to operate as if they were one continuous vessel. The function of end walls, which were the default state in the Devonian, was probably to avoid embolisms. An embolism is where an air bubble is created in a tracheid. This may happen as a result of freezing, or by gases dissolving out of solution. Once an embolism is formed, it usually cannot be removed (but see later); the affected cell cannot pull water up, and is rendered useless.

End walls excluded, the tracheids of prevascular plants were able to operate under the same hydraulic conductivity as those of the first vascular plant, *Cooksonia*.

The size of tracheids is limited as they comprise a single cell; this limits their length, which in turn limits their maximum useful diameter to 80 µm. Conductivity grows with the fourth power of diametre, so increased diametre has huge rewards; vessel elements, consisting of a number of cells, joined at their ends, overcame this limit and allowed larger tubes to form, reaching diameters of up to 500 µm, and lengths of up to 10 m.

Vessels first evolved during the dry, low CO_2 periods of the late Permian, in the horsetails, ferns and Selaginellales independently, and later appeared in the mid Cretaceous in angiosperms and gnetophytes. Vessels allow the same cross-sectional area of wood to transport around a hundred times more water than tracheids! This allowed plants to fill more of their stems with structural fibres, and also opened a new niche to vines, which could transport water without being as thick as the tree they grew on. Despite these advantages, tracheid-based wood is a lot lighter, thus cheaper to make, as vessels need to be much more reinforced to avoid cavitation.

The rhyniophytes of the Rhynie chert comprised nothing more than slender, unornamented axes. The early to middle Devonian trimerophytes, therefore, are the first evidence we have of anything that could be considered leafy. This group of vascular plants are recognisable by their masses of terminal sporangia, which adorn the ends of axes which may bifurcate or trifurcate. Some organisms, such as *Psilophyton*, bore enations. These are small, spiny outgrowths of the stem, lacking their own vascular supply.

Around the same time, the zosterophyllophytes were becoming important. This group is recognisable by their kidney-shaped sporangia, which grew on short lateral branches close to the main axes. They sometimes branched in a distinctive H-shape. The majority of this group bore pronounced spines on their axes. However, none of these had a vascular trace, and the first evidence of vascularised enations occurs in the Rhynie genus *Asteroxylon*. The spines of *Asteroxylon* had a primitive vasuclar supply — at the very least, leaf traces could be seen departing from the central protostele towards each individual 'leaf'. A fossil known as *Baragwanathia* appears in the fossil record slightly earlier, in the late Silurian. In this organism, these leaf traces continue into the leaf to form their mid-vein. One theory, the 'enation theory', holds that the leaves developed by outgrowths of the protostele connecting with existing enations, but it is also possible that microphylls evolved by a branching axis forming 'webbing'.

Asteroxylon and *Baragwanathia* are widely regarded as primitive lycopods The lycopods are still extant today, familiar as the quillwort *Isoetes* and the club mosses. Lycopods bear distinctive microphylls — leaves with a single vascular trace. Microphylls could grow to some size — the Lepidodendrales boasted microphylls over a meter in length — but almost all just bear the one vascular bundle. (An exception is the branching *Selaginella*).

The more familiar leaves, megaphylls, are thought to have separate origins — indeed, they appeared four times independently, in the ferns, horsetails, progymnosperms, and seed plants. They appear to have originated from dichotomising branches, which first overlapped (or 'overtopped') one another, and eventually developed 'webbing' and evolved into gradually more leaf-like structures. So megaphylls, by this 'teleome theory', are composed of a group of webbed branches — hence the 'leaf gap' left where the leaf's vascular bundle leaves that of the main branch resembles two axes splitting. In each of the four groups to evolve megaphylls, their leaves first evolved during the Late Devonian to early Carboniferous, diversifying rapidly until the designs settled down in the mid Carboniferous.

The cessation of further diversification can be attributed to developmental constraints, but why did it take so long for leaves to evolve in the first place? Plants had been on the land for at least 50 million years before megaphylls became significant. However, small, rare mesophylls are known from the early Devonian genus *Eophyllophyton* — so development could not have been a barrier to their appearance. The best explanation so far incorporates observations that atmospheric CO_2 was declining rapidly during this time — falling by around 90 per cent during the Devonian. This corresponded with an increase in stomatal density by 100 times. Stomata allow water to evaporate from leaves, which causes them to curve. It appears that the low stomatal density in the early Devonian meant that evaporation was limited, and leaves would overheat if they grew to any size. The stomatal density could not increase, as the primitive steles and limited root systems would not be able to supply water quickly enough to match the rate of transpiration.

Clearly, leaves are not always beneficial, as illustrated by the frequent occurrence of secondary loss of leaves, famously exemplified by cacti and the 'whisk fern' *Psilotum.*

Secondary evolution can also disguise the true evolutionary origin of some leaves. Some genera of ferns display complex leaves which are attached to the pseudostele by an outgrowth of the vascular bundle, leaving no leaf gap. Further, horsetail (*Equisetum*) leaves bear only a single vein, and appear for all the world to be microphyllous; however, in the light of the fossil record and molecular evidence, we conclude that their forbears bore leaves with complex venation, and the current state is a result of secondary simplification.

Deciduous trees deal with another disadvantage to having leaves. The popular belief that plants shed their leaves when the days get too short is misguided; evergreens prospered in the Arctic circle during the most recent greenhouse earth. The generally accepted reason for shedding leaves during winter is to cope with the weather — the force of wind and weight of snow are much more comfortably weathered without leaves to increase surface area. Seasonal leaf loss has evolved independently several times and is exhibited in the ginkgoales, pinophyta and angiosperms Leaf loss may also have arisen as a response to pressure from insects; it may have been less costly to lose leaves entirely during the winter or dry season than to continue investing resources in their repair.

Evolution of Trees

The early Devonian landscape was devoid of vegetation taller than waist height. Without the evolution of a robust vascular system, taller heights could not be obtained. There was, however, a constant evolutionary pressure to attain greater height. The most obvious advantage is the harvesting of more sunlight for photosynthesis — by overshadowing competitors — but a further advantage is present in spore distribution, as spores (and, later, seeds) can be blown greater distances if they start higher. This may be demonstrated by *Prototaxites*, thought to be a late Silurian fungus reaching eight metres in height.

In order to attain arborescence, early plants needed to develop woody tissue that would act as both support and water transport. To understand wood, we must know a little of vascular behaviour. The stele of plants undergoing 'secondary growth' is surrounded by the vascular cambium, a ring of cells which produces more xylem (on the inside) and phloem (on the outside). Since xylem cells comprise dead, lignified tissue, subsequent rings of xylem are added to those already present, forming wood.

The first plants to develop this secondary growth, and a woody habit, were apparently the ferns, and as early as the middle Devonian one species, *Wattieza*, had already reached heights of 8 m and a tree-like habit.

Other clades did not take long to develop a tree-like stature; the late Devonian *Archaeopteris*, a precursor to gymnosperms which evolved from the trimerophytes reached 30 m in height. These progymnosperms were the first plants to develop true wood, grown from a bifacial cambium, of which the first appearance is in the mid Devonian *Rellimia*. True wood is only thought to have evolved once, giving rise to the concept of a 'lignophyte' clade.

These *Archaeopteris* forests were soon supplemented by lycopods, in the form of lepidodendrales, which topped 50m in height and 2m across at the base. These lycopods rose to dominate late Devonian and Carboniferous coal deposits. Lepidodendrales differ from modern trees in exhibiting determinate growth: after building up a reserve of nutrients at a low height, the plants would 'bolt' to a genetically determined height, branch at that level, spread their spores and die. They consisted of 'cheap' wood to allow their rapid growth, with at least half of their stems comprising a pith-filled cavity. Their wood was also generated by a unifacial vascular cambium — it did not produce new phloem, meaning that the trunks could not grow wider over time.

The horsetail *Calamites* was next on the scene, appearing in the Carboniferous. Unlike the modern horsetail *Equisetum*, *Calamites* had a unifacial vascular cambium, allowing them to develop wood and grow to heights in excess of 10 m. They also branched multiple times.

While the form of early trees was similar to that of today's, the groups containing all modern trees had yet to evolve.

The dominant groups today are the gymnosperms, which include the coniferous trees, and the angiosperms, which contain all fruiting and flowering trees. It was long thought that the angiosperms arose from within the gymnosperms, but recent molecular evidence suggests that their living representatives form two distinct groups. It must be noted that the molecular data has yet to be fully reconciled with morphological data but it is becoming accepted that the morphological support for paraphyly is not especially strong. This would lead to the conclusion that both groups arose from within the pteridosperms, probably as early as the Permian.

The angiosperms and their ancestors played a very small role until they diversified during the Cretaceous. They started out as small, damp-loving organisms in the understory, and have been diversifying ever since the mid-Cretaceous, to become the dominant member of non-boreal forests today.

Evolution of Roots

The roots (bottom image) of lepidodendrales are thought to be functionally equivalent to the stems (top), as the similar appearance of 'leaf scars' and 'root scars' on these specimens from different species demonstrates.

Roots are important to plants for two main reasons: Firstly, they provide anchorage to the substrate; more importantly, they provide a source of water and nutrients from the soil. Roots allowed plants to grow taller and faster.

The onset of roots also had effects on a global scale. By disturbing the soil, and promoting its acidification (by taking up nutrients such as nitrate and phosphate they enabled it to weather more deeply, promoting the draw-down of CO_2 with huge implications for climate. These effects may have been so profound they led to a mass extinction.

But how and when did roots evolve in the first place? While there are traces of root-like impressions in fossil soils in the late Silurian, body fossils show the earliest plants to be devoid of roots. Many had tendrils which sprawled along or beneath the ground, with upright axes or thalli dotted here and there, and some even had non-photosynthetic subterranean branches which lacked stomata. The distinction between root and specialised branch is developmental; true roots follow a different developmental trajectory to stems. Further, roots differ in their branching pattern, and in possession of a root cap So while Silu-

Devonian plants such as *Rhynia* and *Horneophyton* possessed the physiological equivalent of roots, roots — defined as organs differentiated from stems — did not arrive until later. Unfortunately, roots are rarely preserved in the fossil record, and our understanding of their evolutionary origin is sparse.

Rhizoids — small structures performing the same role as roots, usually a cell in diametre — probably evolved very early, perhaps even before plants colonised the land; they are recognised in the Characeae, an algal sister group to land plants. That said, rhizoids probably evolved more than once; the rhizines of lichens, for example, perform a similar role. Even some animals (*Lamellibrachia*) have root-like structures!

More advanced structures are common in the Rhynie chert, and many other fossils of comparable early Devonian age bear structures that look like, and acted like, roots. The rhyniophytes bore fine rhizoids, and the trimerophytes and herbaceous lycopods of the chert bore root-like structure penetrating a few centimetres into the soil. However, none of these fossils display all the features borne by modern roots. Roots and root-like structures became increasingly more common and deeper penetrating during the Devonian period, with lycopod trees forming roots around 20 cm long during the Eifelian and Givetian. These were joined by progymnosperms, which rooted up to about a metre deep, during the ensuing Frasnian stage. True gymnosperms and zygopterid ferns also formed shallow rooting systems during the Famennian period.

The rhizomorphs of the lycopods provide a slightly approach to rooting. They were equivalent to stems, with organs equivalent to leaves performing the role of rootlets. A similar construction is observed in the extant lycopod *Isoetes*, and this appears to be evidence that roots evolved independently at least twice, in the lycophytes and other plants.

A vascular system is indispensable to a rooted plants, as non-photosynthesising roots need a supply of sugars, and a vascular system is required to transport water and nutrients from the roots to the rest of the plant. These plants are little more advanced than their Silurian forbears, without a dedicated root system; however, the flat-lying axes can be clearly seen to have growths similar to the rhizoids of bryophytes today.

By the mid-to-late Devonian, most groups of plants had independently developed a rooting system of some nature. As roots became larger, they could support larger trees, and the soil was weathered to a greater depth. This deeper weathering had effects not only on the aforementioned drawdown of CO_2, but also opened up new habitats for colonisation by fungi and animals.

Roots today have developed to the physical limits. They penetrate many metres of soil to tap the water table. The narrowest roots are a mere 40 μm in diameter, and could not physically transport water if they were any narrower. The earliest fossil roots recovered, by contrast, narrowed from 3 mm to under 700 μm in diameter; of course, taphonomy is the ultimate control of what thickness we can see.

Arbuscular Mycorrhizae

The efficiency of many plants' roots is increased via a symbiotic relationship with a fungal partner. The most common are arbuscular mycorrhizae (AM), literally 'tree-like fungal roots'. These comprise fungi which invade some root cells, filling the cell membrane with their hyphae. They feed on the plant's sugars, but return nutrients generated or extracted from the soil (especially phosphate), which the plant would otherwise have no access to.

This symbiosis appears to have evolved early in plant history. AM are found in all plant groups, and 80 per cent of extant vascular plants, suggesting an early ancestry; a 'plant'-fungus symbiosis may even have been the step that enabled them to colonise the land, and indeed AM are abundant in the Rhynie chert; the association occurred even before there were true roots to colonise, and is has even been suggested that roots evolved in order to provide a more comfortable habitat for mycorrhizal fungi.

Evolution of Seeds

Early land plants reproduced in the fashion of ferns: spores germinated into small gametophytes, which produced sperm. These would swim across moist soils to find the female organs (archegonia) on the same or another gametophyte, where they would fuse with an ovule to produce an embryo, which would germinate into a sporophyte.

This mode of reproduction restricted early plants to damp environments, moist enough that the sperm could swim to their destination. Therefore, early land plants were constrained to the lowlands, near shores and streams. The development of heterospory freed them from this constraint.

Heterosporic organisms, as their name suggests, bear spores of two sizes — microspores and megaspores. These would germinate to form microgametophytes and megagametophytes, respectively. This system paved the way for seeds: taken to the extreme, the megasporangia could bear only a single megaspore tetrad, and to complete the transition to true seeds, three of the megaspores in the original tetrad could be aborted, leaving one megaspore per megasporangium.

The transition to seeds continued with this megaspore being 'boxed in' to its sporangium while it germinates. Then, the megagametophyte is contained within a waterproof integuement, which forms the bulk of the seed. The microgametophyte — a pollen grain which has germinated from a microspore — is employed for dispersal, only releasing its desiccation-prone sperm when it reaches a receptive microgametophyte.

Lycopods go a fair way down the path to seeds without ever crossing the threshold. Fossil lycopod megaspores reaching 1 cm in diametre, and surrounded by vegetative tissue, are known — these even germinate into a megagametophyte *in situ*. However, they fall short of being seeds, since the nucellus, an inner spore-covering layer, does not completely enclose the spore. A very small slit remains, meaning that the seed is still exposed to the atmosphere. This has two consequences — firstly, it means it is not fully resistant to desiccation, and secondly, sperm do not have to 'burrow' to access the archegonia of the megaspore.

The first 'spermatophytes' (literally:seed plants) — that is, the first plants to bear true seeds — were progymnosperms called pteridosperms: literally, 'seed ferns'. They ranged from trees to small, rambling shrubs; like most early progymnosperms, they were woody plants with fern-like foliage. They all bore ovules, but no cones, fruit or similar. While it is difficult to track the early evolution of seeds, we can trace the lineage of the seed ferns from the simple trimerophytes through homosporous Aneurophytes.

This seed model is shared by basically all gymnosperms (literally: 'naked seeds'), most of which encase their seeds in a woody or fleshy (the yew, for example) cone, but none of which fully enclose their seeds. The angiosperms ('vessel seeds') are the only group to fully enclose the seed, in a carpel.

Fully enclosed seeds opened up a new pathway for plants to follow: that of seed dormancy. The embryo, completely isolated from the external atmosphere and hence protected from desiccation, could survive some years of drought before germinating. Gymnosperm seeds from the late Carboniferous have been found to contain embryos, suggesting a lengthy gap between fertilisation and germination. This period is associated with the entry into a greenhouse earth period, with an associated increase in aridity. This suggests that dormancy arose as a response to drier climatic conditions, where it became advantageous to wait for a moist period before germinating. This evolutionary breakthrough appears to have opened a floodgate: previously inhospitable areas, such as dry mountain slopes, could now be tolerated, as were soon covered by trees.

Seeds offered further advantages to their bearers: they increased the success rate of fertilised gametophytes, and because a nutrient store could be 'packaged' in with the embryo, the seeds could germinate rapidly in inhospitable environments, reaching a size where it could fend for itself more quickly. For example, without an endosperm, seedlings growing in arid environments would not have the reserves to grow roots deep enough to reach the water table before they expired. Likewise, seeds germinating in a gloomy understory require an additional reserve of energy to quickly grow high enough to capture sufficient light for self-sustenance. A combination of these advantages gave seed plants the ecological edge over the previously dominant genus *Archaeopteris*, this increasing the biodiversity of early forests.

The relationship of stem groups to the angiosperms is of utmost importance in determining the evolution of flowers; stem groups provide an insight into the state of earlier "forks" on the path to the current state. If we identify an unrelated group as a stem group, then we will gain an incorrect image of the lineages' history. The traditional view that flowers arose by modification of a structure similar to that of the gnetales, for example, no longer bears weight in the light of the molecular data.

Convergence increases our chances of misidentifying stem groups. Since the protection of the megagametophyte is evolutionarily desirable, it would be unsurprising if many separate groups stumbled upon protective encasements independently. Distinguishing ancestry in such a situation, especially where we usually only have fossils to go on, is tricky — to say the least.

In flowers, this protection is offered by the carpel, an organ believed to represent an adapted leaf, recruited into a protective role, shielding the ovules. These ovules are further protected by a double-walled integument.

Penetration of these protective layers needs something more that a free-floating microgametophyte. Angiosperms have pollen grains comprising just three cells. One cell is responsible for drilling down through the integuments, and creating a conduit for the two sperm cells to flow down. The megagametophyte has just seven cells; of these, one fuses with a sperm cell, forming the nucleus of the egg itself, and another joins with the other sperm, and dedicates itself to forming a nutrient-rich endosperm. The other cells take auxiliary roles. This process of 'double fertilisation' is unique and common to all angiosperms. However, no true flowers are found in any groups save those extant today. Most morphological and molecular analyses place *Amborella*, the nymphaeales and Austrobaileyaceae in a basal clade dubbed 'ANA'. This clade appear to have diverged in the early Cretaceous, around 130 million years ago — around the same time as the earliest fossil angiosperm, and just after the first angiosperm-like pollen, 136 million years ago. The magnoliids diverged soon after, and a rapid radiation had produced eudicots and monocots by 125 million years ago. By the end of the Cretaceous 65.5 million years ago, over 50 per cent of today's angiosperm orders had evolved, and the clade accounted for 70 per cent of global species. It was around this time that flowering trees became dominant over conifers.

The features of the basal 'ANA' groups suggest that angiosperms originated in dark, damp, frequently disturbed areas. It appears that the angiosperms remained constrained to such habitats throughout the Cretaceous — occupying the niche of small herbs early in the successional series. This may have restricted their initial significance, but given them the flexibility that accounted for the rapidity of their later diversifications in other habitats.

The most recent major innovation by the plants is the development of the C_4 metabolic pathway.

Photosynthesis is not quite as simple as adding water to CO_2 to produce sugars and oxygen. A complex chemical pathway is involved, facilitated along the way by a range of enzymes and co-enzymes. The enzyme RuBisCO is responsible for "fixing" CO_2 — that is, it attaches it to a carbon-based molecule to form a sugar, which can be used by the plant, releasing an oxygen molecule along the way. However, the enzyme is notoriously inefficient, and just as effectively will also fix oxygen instead of CO_2 in a process called photorespiration. This is energetically costly as the plant has to use energy to turn the products of photorepsiration back into a form that can react with CO_2.

A second method, CAM photosynthesis, temporally separates photosynthesis from the action of RuBisCO. RuBisCO only operates during the day, when stomata are sealed and CO_2 is provided by the breakdown of the chemical malate. More CO_2 is then harvested from the atmosphere when stomata open, during the cool, moist nights, reducing water loss.

Evolutionary Record

These two pathways, with the same effect on RuBisCO, evolved a number of times independently — indeed, C_4 alone arose in 18 different plant families. The C_4 construction is most famously used by a subset of grasses, while CAM is employed by many succulents and cacti. The trait appears to have emerged during the Oligocene, around 25 to 32 million years ago; however, they did not become ecologically significant until the Miocene, -1 million years ago. Remarkably, some charcoalified fossils preserve tissue organised into the Kranz anatomy, with intact bundle sheath cells, allowing the presence C_4 metabolism to be identified without doubt at this time. In deducing their distribution and significance, we resort to the use of isotopic markers. C_3 plants preferentially use the lighter of two isotopes of carbon in the atmosphere, ^{12}C, which is more readily involved in the chemical pathways involved in its fixation. Because C_4 metabolism involves a further chemical step, this effect is accentuated. Plant material can be analysed to deduce the ratio of the heavier ^{13}C to ^{12}C. This ratio is denoted $d^{13}C$. C_3 plants are on average around 14‰ (parts per thousand) lighter than the atmospheric ratio, while C_4 plants are about 28 per cent lighter. The $d^{13}C$ of CAM plants depends on the percentage of carbon fixed at night relative to what is fixed in the day, being closer to C_3 plants if they fix most carbon in the day and closer to C_4 plants if they fix all their carbon at night.

It's troublesome procuring original fossil material in sufficient quantity to analyse the grass itself, but fortunately we have a good proxy: horses. Horses were globally widespread in the period of interest, and browsed almost exclusively on grasses. There's an old phrase in isotope palæontology, "you are what you eat (plus a little bit)" — this refers to the fact that organisms reflect the isotopic composition of whatever they eat, plus a small adjustment factor. There is a good record of horse teeth throughout the globe, and their $d^{13}C$ has been measured. The record shows a sharp negative inflection around -1 million years ago, during the Messinian, and this is interpreted as the rise of C_4 plants on a global scale.

Concentrating Carbon

To work around this inefficiency, C_4 plants evolved carbon concentrating mechanisms. These work by increasing the concentration of CO_2 around RuBisCO, thereby increasing the amount of photosynthesis and decreasing photorespiration. The process of concentrating CO_2 around RuBisCO requires more energy than allowing gases to diffuse, but under certain conditions — i.e. warm temperatures (>25°C), low CO_2 concentrations, or high oxygen concentrations — pays off in terms of the decreased loss of sugars through photorespiration.

One, C_4 metabolism, employs a so-called Kranz anatomy. This transports CO_2 through an outer mesophyll layer, via a range of organic molecules, to the central bundle sheath cells, where the CO_2 is released. In this way, CO_2 is concentrated near the site of RuBisCO operation. Because RuBisCO is operating in an environment with much more CO_2 than it otherwise would be, it performs more efficiently.

In the fossil record, there are three intriguing groups which bore flower-like structures. The first is the Permian pteridosperm *Glossopteris*, which already bore recurved leaves resembling carpels. The Triassic *Caytonia* is more flower-like still, with enclosed ovules — but only a single integument. Further, details of their pollen and stamens set them apart from true flowering plants.

The Bennettitales bore remarkably flower-like organs, protected by whorls of bracts which may have played a similar role to the petals and sepals of true flowers; however, these flower-like structures evolved independently, as the Bennettitales are more closely related to cycads and ginkgos than to the angiosperms.

The evolution of syncarps:

(a) sporangia borne at tips of leaf;

(b) Leaf curls up to protect sporangia;

(c) leaf curls to form enclosed roll; and

(d) grouping of three rolls into a syncarp.

Flowers are modified leaves possessed only by the group known as the angiosperms, which are relatively late to appear in the fossil record. Colourful and/or pungent structures surround the cones of plants such as cycads and gnetales, making a strict definition of the term ‘flower’ elusive.

The flowering plants have long been assumed to have evolved from within the *gymnosperms*; according to the traditional morphological view, they are closely allied to the gnetales. However, as noted above, recent molecular evidence is at odds to this hypothesis, and further suggests that gnetales are more closely related to some gymnosperm groups than angiosperms, and that extant gymnosperms form a distinct clade to the angiosperms, the two clades diverging some 300 million years ago.

When is C_4 an advantage?

While C_4 enhances the efficiency of RuBisCO, the concentration of carbon is highly energy intensive. This means that C_4 plants only have an advantage over C_3 organisms in certain conditions: namely, high temperatures and low rainfall. C_4 plants also need high levels of sunlight in order to thrive Models suggest that without wildfires removing shade-casting trees and shrubs, there would be no space for C_4 plants. But wildfires have occurred for 400 million years — why did C_4 take so long to arise, and then appear independently so many times? The Carboniferous period (~300 million years ago) had notoriously high oxygen levels — almost enough to allow spontaneous combustion — and very low CO_2, but there is no C_4 isotopic signature to be found. And there doesn't seem to be a sudden trigger for the Miocene rise.

During the Micoene, the atmosphere and climate was relatively stable. If anything, it increased gradually from 14 to 9 million years ago before settling down to concentrations similar to the Holocene. This suggests that it did not have a key role in invoking C_4 evolution. Grasses themselves (the group which would give rise to the most occurrences of C_4) had probably been around for 60 million years or more, so had had plenty of time to evolve C_4 which in any case is present in a diverse range of groups and thus evolved independently. There is a strong signal of climate change in South Asia; increasing aridity — hence increasing fire frequency and intensity — may have led to an increase in the importance of grasslands. However, this is difficult to reconcile with the North American record. It is possible that the signal is entirely biological, forced by the fire- (and elephant?)- driven acceleration of grass evolution — which, both by increasing weathering and incorporating more carbon into sediments, reduced atmospheric CO_2 levels. Finally, there is evidence that the onset of C_4 from 9 to 7 million years ago is a biased signal, which only holds true for North America, from where most samples originate; emerging evidence suggests that grasslands evolved to a dominant state at least 15Ma earlier in South America.

Evolutionary Trends

The process of evolution works slightly differently in plants than animals. Differences in plant physiology and reproduction mean that while the same evolutionary principles of natural selection apply, the finer nuances of their effect are radically different.

One major difference is the ability of plants to reproduce clonally, and the totipotent nature of their cells, allowing them to reproduce asexually much more easily than most animals. They are also capable of polyploidy — where more than two chromosome sets are inherited from parents. This allows relatively fast bursts of evolution to occur. The long periods of dormancy that seed plants can employ also makes them less vulnerable to extinction, as they can 'sit out' the tough periods and wait until more clement times to leap back to life.

The effect of these differences is most profoundly seen during extinction events. These events, which wiped out between 6 and 62 per cent of terrestrial animal families, had 'negligible' effect on plant families. However, the ecosystem structure is significantly rearranged, with the abundances and distributions of different groups of plants changing profoundly. These effects are perhaps due to the higher diversity within families, as extinction — which *was* common at the species level — was very selective. For example, wind-pollinated species survived better than insect-pollinated taxa, and specialised species generally lost out. In general, the surviving taxa were rare before the extinction, suggesting that they were generalists who were poor competitors when times were easy, but prospered when specialised groups went extinct and left ecological niches vacant.

Viticulture

Viticulture (from the Latin word for *vine*) is the science, production and study of grapes which deals with the series of events that occur in the vineyard. When the grapes are used for winemaking, it is also known as viniculture. It is one branch of the science of horticulture.

While the native territory of *Vitis vinifera*, the common grape vine, is a band of area from Western Europe to the Persian shores of the Caspian Sea, the vine has demonstrated high levels of adaptability and will sometimes mutate to accommodate a new environment after its introduction. Because of this Viticulture can be found on every continent except Antarctica.

Duties of the viticulturist include: monitoring and controlling pests and diseases, fertilizing, irrigation, canopy management, monitoring fruit development and characteristics, deciding when to harvest and vine pruning during the winter months. Viticulturists are often intimately involved with winemakers, because vineyard management and the resulting grape characteristics, provide the basis from which winemaking can begin.

The history of viticulture is closely related to the history of wine with evidence of man cultivating wild grapes to make wine dating as far back as the Neolithic period. There is evidence that some of the earliest domestication of *Vitis vinifera* occurred in the area of the modern day country Georgia. There is also evidence of grape domestication occurring Near East in the Early Bronze Age around 3200 BC.

The earliest act of cultivation appears to have been the favoring of Hermaphroditic members of the *Vitis vinifera* species over the barren male vines and the female vines which were dependent on having a nearby male to pollinate. With the ability to pollinate itself, over time the hermaphroditic vines were able to sire offspring that was consistently hermaphroditic itself.

At the end of the 5th century BC, the Greek historian Thucydides wrote:

> "The people of the Mediterranean began to emerge from barbarism when they learnt to cultivate the olive and the vine".

The time period that Thucydides was most likely referencing was the time between 3000 BC and 2000 BC when viticulture emerged in force in the areas of Asia Minor, Crete, Greece and the Cyclades of the Aegean Sea. It was during this period that grape cultivation moved from being just an aspect of local consumption to an important component of local economies and trade.

Roman Viticulture

Between 1200 BC to 900 BC the Phoenician developed viticulture practices that were later utilized in Carthage. Around 500 BC, the Carthaginian writer Mago recorded these practices in 28 volume work that was one of the few artifacts to survive the Roman destruction of Carthage during the Third Punic War. The Roman statesman Cato the Elder was influenced by these text and around 160 BC wrote *De Agri Cultura* which expounded on Roman viticulture and agriculture. The Roman writer Columella produced the most detailed work on Roman viticulture with his twelve volume AD 65 text *De Re Rustica*. Columella work is one of the earliest to detail trellis systems for getting vines off the ground. Columella advocated the use of stakes versus the previously accepted practice of training the vines to grow up along tree trunks. The benefits of using stakes over trees was largely to minimize the dangers associated with climbing trees to prune the dense foliage to give the vines sunlight and later to harvest.

Roman expansion across Western Europe also brought Roman viticulture to the areas that would be home to some of the world most well known wine-growing regions—the Spanish Rioja, the German Mosel, and the French Bordeaux, Burgundy and Rhône. Romans viticulturists were among the first to identify steep hillsides as one of the more ideal locations to plant vines because cool air runs downhill and gathers at the bottom of valleys. While some cool air is beneficial, too much can rob the vine of the heat it needs for photosynthesis and in the wintertime increase the hazard for frost.

Mediaeval Viticulture

In the Middle Ages, Catholic monks (particularly the Cistercians) were the most prominent viticulturists of the time period. Around this time, an early system of *Metayage* emerged in France with labourers (*Prendeur*) working the vineyards under contractual agreements with the landowners (*Bailleur*). In most cases, the *prendeurs* were giving flexibility in selecting their crop and developing their own vineyard practice.

Many of the viticultural practices developed in this time period would become staples of European viticulture till the 18th century. Varietals were studied more intently to see which vines were the most suitable for a particular area. Around this time an early concept of *terroir* emerged as wines from particular places began to develop a reputation for uniqueness. The concept of pruning for quality over quantity emerged though it would create conflict between the rich landowners who wanted higher quality wines and the peasant labourers who livelihood dependent on the quantity of wine they could sell. The Riesling is the famous example for higher quality of wine. In 1435 Count John IV. of Katzenelnbogen started this successful tradition.

In Burgundy, the Cistercian monks developed the concept of *cru* vineyards as homogeneous pieces of land that consistently produce wines each vintage that are similar. In areas like the Côte-d'Or the monks divided the land into separate vineyards, many of which are still around today—like Montrachet and La Romanée.

Growing Vines

The vast majority of the world's wine producing regions are found between the temperate latitudes of 30° and 50° in both hemispheres. In these bands the annual mean temperatures are between 10 and 20 °C (50 and 68 °F). The presence of large bodies of water and mountain ranges can have positive effects on the climate and vines. Nearby lakes and rivers can serve as protection for drastic temperature drops at night by releasing the heat it has stored during the day to warm the vines. The vine needs approximately 1300-1500 hours of sunshine during the growing season and around 690 millimetres (27′) of rainfall throughout the year in order to produce grapes suitable for winemaking. In ideal circumstances the vine will receive most of the rainfall during the winter and spring months. Rain during the harvest time can create many hazards such as fungal diseases and berries splitting. The optimum weather during the growing season is a long, warm summer that allows the grapes the opportunity to fully ripen and develop a balance between the acid and sugar levels in the grape.

Other factors that viticulturists consider is the topography of the area with hillsides and slopes being preferred over flatter terrain. A main reason for this is that vines on an angle can receive a greater strength of the sun rays with the sunshine falling on a perpendicular angle to the slope. With flatter terrain, the strength of the sunlight is diluted as it is spread out across a wider surface area. An additional benefit is the natural drainage that a slope offers so that the vine doesn't sit with too much moisture in the soil. In cooler climate regions of the northern hemisphere, South facing slopes receive more hours of sunlight and are preferred. In warmer climates, north facing slopes are preferred. (In the southern hemisphere these orientations are reversed).

Hazards

There are many hazards that a viticulturist needs to be aware of when growing vines. These hazards can have an adverse effect on the wine produced from the grape or kill the vine itself. When the vine is flowering it is very susceptible to weather hazards such as strong winds and hail. Cold temperatures during this period can also bring the onset of *millerandage* which produces clusters with no seeds and varying sizes. Too much heat can have the opposite reaction and produce Coulure that causes grape clusters to either drop to the ground or not fully develop.

A *green harvest* is the removal of immature grape bunches, typically for the purpose of decreasing yield. In French it is known as a *vendange verte*.

Green harvesting is a relatively modern practice most often used to produce fine wine. Removing the tiny, immature grapes while they are still green induces the vine to put all its energy into developing the remaining grapes. In theory this results in better ripening and the development of more numerous and mature flavour compounds. In the absence of a green harvest, a healthy, vigorous vine can produce dilute, unripe grapes.

Many traditionally renowned regions have natural conditions that suppress excess vigor. Examples include the gravelly soil of Bordeaux, the often cool climate of Burgundy, and the meager rainfall of Rioja. In these regions, the vine is prevented from producing too many grapes without human intervention. However, in regions with fertile soil, copious sunlight, and irrigation, the vine can generate huge quantities of characterless grapes. One solution is a green harvest. After fruit set, the quantity of grapes that will result from a vineyard can be estimated. Often the grower has a target yield in mind, measured in tons per acre or hectoliters per hectare. A portion of the grape bunches are cut off, to leave approximately the correct amount.

In Europe, many appellations restrict the yield permitted from a given area, so there is even more incentive to perform green harvesting when presented with excess crop. Often the excess must be sold for a pittance and used for industrial alcohol production rather than wine.

While the concept of thinning or sacrificing part of the grape crop, i.e. green harvesting, with the aim of improving the quality of the remaining grapes, predates modern critics, the practice has increased in recent times in vineyards found in California and areas where the grapes grow easily.

A field blend is a wine that is produced from two or more different grape varieties inter planted in the same vineyard. In the days before precise varietal identification, let alone rigorous clonal selection, a vineyard might be planted by taking cuttings from another vineyard and therefore approximately copying its genetic makeup. This meant that one vine could be Zinfandel and the next Carignan. When making wine with little equipment to spare for separate vinification of different varieties, field blends allowed effortless, though inflexible, blending.

Fermentation tanks are now cheap enough that the field blend is an anachronism, and almost all wines are assembled by blending from smaller, individual lots. However, in California some of the oldest (and lowest-yielding) Zinfandel comes from vineyards that are field-blended. Ridge Vineyards owns the Lytton Springs vineyards in Sonoma County, which were planted from 1900 to 1905 in what Ridge calls "a traditional field blend of about seventy per cent Zinfandel, twenty per cent Petite Sirah, and ten per cent Grenache and Carignan."

Gemischter Satz is a wine term in German equivalent to a field blend, which means that grapes of different varieties are planted, harvested and vinified together. In older times, this was common, but the practice has almost stopped.

Plant Science

Plant science(s), *phytology*, or *plant biology* is a branch of biology and is the scientific study of plant life and development. Botany covers a wide range of scientific disciplines that study plants, algae, and fungi including: structure, growth, reproduction, metabolism, development, diseases, chemical properties, and evolutionary relationships between the different groups. Botany began with early human efforts to identify edible, medicinal and poisonous plants, making botany one of the oldest sciences. From this ancient interest in plants, the scope of botany has increased to include the study of over 5,50,000 species of living organisms.

As with other life forms in biology, plant life can be studied from different perspectives, from the molecular, genetic and biochemical level through organelles, cells, tissues, organs, individuals, plant populations, and communities of plants. At each of these levels a botanist might be concerned with the classification (taxonomy), structure (anatomy and morphology), or function (physiology) of plant life.

Historically all living things were grouped as animals or plants, and botany covered all organisms not considered animals. Some organisms once included in the field of botany are no longer considered to belong to the plant kingdom — these include fungi (studied in mycology), lichens (lichenology), bacteria (bacteriology), viruses (virology) and single-celled algae, which are now grouped as part of the Protista. However, attention is still given to these groups by botanists, and fungi, lichens, bacteria and photosynthetic protists are usually covered in introductory botany courses.

The study of plants is vital because they are a fundamental part of life on Earth, which generates the oxygen, food, fibres, fuel and medicine that allow humans and other life forms to exist. Through photosynthesis, plants absorb carbon dioxide, a greenhouse gas that in large amounts can affect global climate. Additionally, they prevent soil erosion and are influential in the water cycle. A good understanding of plants is crucial to the future of human societies as it allows us to:

- Produce food to feed an expanding population;
- Understand fundamental life processes;
- Produce medicine and materials to treat diseases and other ailments;
- Understand environmental changes more clearly.

Paleobotanists study ancient plants in the fossil record. It is believed that early in the Earth's history, the evolution of photosynthetic plants altered the global atmosphere of the earth, changing the ancient atmosphere by oxidation.

Human Nutrition

Nearly all the food we eat comes (directly and indirectly) from plants like this American long grain rice.

Virtually all foods eaten come from plants, either directly from staple foods and other fruit and vegetables, or indirectly through livestock or other animals, which rely on plants for their nutrition. Plants are the fundamental base of nearly all food chains because they use the energy from the sun and nutrients from the soil and atmosphere, converting them into a form that can be consumed and utilized by animals; this is what ecologists call the first trophic level. Botanists also study how plants produce food we can eat and how to increase yields and therefore their work is important in mankind's ability to feed the world and provide food security for future generations, for example, through plant breeding. Botanists also study weeds, plants which are considered to be a nuisance in a particular location. Weeds are a considerable problem in agriculture, and botany provides some of the basic science used to understand how to minimize 'weed' impact in agriculture and native ecosystems. Ethnobotany is the study of the relationships between plants and people.

Fundamental Life Processes

Plants are convenient organisms in which fundamental life processes (like cell division and protein synthesis) can be studied, without the ethical dilemmas of studying animals or humans. The genetic laws of inheritance were discovered in this way by Gregor Mendel, who was studying the way pea shape is inherited. What Mendel learned from studying plants has had far reaching benefits outside of botany. Additionally, Barbara McClintock discovered 'jumping genes' by studying maize. These are a few examples that demonstrate how botanical research has an ongoing relevance to the understanding of fundamental biological processes.

Medicine and Materials

Many medicinal and recreational drugs, like tetrahydrocannabinol, caffeine, and nicotine come directly from the plant kingdom. Others are simple derivatives of botanical natural products; for example, aspirin is based on the pain killer salicylic acid which originally came from the bark of willow trees. As well, the narcotic analgesics such as morphine are derived from the opium poppy. There may be many novel cures for diseases provided by plants, waiting to be discovered. Popular stimulants like coffee, chocolate, tobacco, and tea also come from plants. Most alcoholic beverages come from fermenting plants such as barley (beer), rice (sake) and grapes (wine).

Plants also provide us with many natural materials, such as hemp, cotton, wood, paper, linen, vegetable oils, some types of rope, and rubber. The production of silk would not be possible without the cultivation of the mulberry plant. Sugarcane, rapeseed, soy and other plants with a highly-fermentable sugar or oil content have recently been put to use as sources of biofuels, which are important alternatives to fossil fuels (see biodiesel).

Environmental Changes

Plants can also help us understand changes in on our environment in many ways:

- Understanding habitat destruction and species extinction is dependent on an accurate and complete catalog of plant systematics and taxonomy.
- Plant responses to ultraviolet radiation can help us monitor problems like ozone depletion.
- Analyzing pollen deposited by plants thousands or millions of years ago can help scientists to reconstruct past climates and predict future ones, an essential part of climate change research.
- Recording and analyzing the timing of plant life cycles are important parts of phenology used in climate-change research.
- Lichens, which are sensitive to atmospheric conditions, have been extensively used as pollution indicators.

In many different ways, plants can act a little like the 'miners' canary', an early warning system alerting us to important changes in our environment. In addition to these practical and scientific reasons, plants are extremely valuable as recreation for millions of people who enjoy gardening, horticultural and culinary uses of plants every day.

Early examples of plant taxonomy occur in the Rigveda, that divides plants into *V?ska* (tree), *Osadhi* (herbs useful to humans) and *Virudha* (creepers), which are then further subdivided. The Atharvaveda divides plants into eight classes, *Visakha* (spreading branches), *Manjari* (leaves with long clusters), *Sthambini* (bushy plants), *Prastanavati* (which expands); *Ekas?nga* (those with monopodial growth), *Pratanavati* (creeping plants), *Amsumati* (with many stalks), and *Kandini* (plants with knotty joints). The Taittiriya Samhita classifies the plant kingdom into *v?ksa*, *vana* and *druma* (trees), *visakha* (shrubs with spreading branches), *sasa* (herbs), *amsumali* (a spreading or deliquescent plant), *vratati* (climber), *stambini* (bushy plant), *pratanavati* (creeper), and *alasala* (those spreading on the ground).

Manusmriti – Law book of Hindus — proposed a classification of plants in eight major categories. Charaka Samhita and Sushruta Samhita and the Vaisesikas also present an elaborate taxonomy.

Parashara, the author of *V?ksayurveda* (the science of life of trees), classifies plants into Dvimatrka (Dicotyledons) and Ekamatrka (Monocotyledons). These are further classified into *Samiganiya* (Fabaceae), *Puplikagalniya* (Rutaceae), *Svastikaganiya* (Cruciferae), *Tripuspaganiya* (Cucurbitaceae), *Mallikaganiya* (Apocynaceae), and *Kurcapuspaganiya* (Asteraceae).

Important mediaeval Indian works of plant physiology include the *Prthviniraparyam* of Udayana, *Nyayavindutika* of Dharmottara, *Saddarsana-samuccaya* of Gunaratna, and *Upaskara* of Sankaramisra.

In ancient China, the recorded listing of different plants and herb concoctions for pharmaceutical purposes spans back to at least the Warring States (481 BC-221 BC). Many Chinese writers over the centuries contributed to the written knowledge of herbal pharmaceutics. There was the Han Dynasty (202 BC-220 AD) written work of the Huangdi Neijing and the famous pharmacologist Zhang Zhongjing of the 2nd century. There was also the 11th century scientists and statesmen Su Song and Shen Kuo, who compiled treatises on herbal medicine and included the use of mineralogy.

Greco-Roman World

Among the earliest of botanical works in Europe, written around 300 B.C., are two large treatises by Theophrastus: *On the History of Plants* (*Historia Plantarum*) and *On the Causes of Plants.* Together these books constitute the most important contribution to botanical science during antiquity and on into the Middle Ages. Aristotle also wrote about plants. One theory about plants that Greco-Romans came up with about plants was that they ate soil for nutrients.

The Roman medical writer Pedanius Dioscorides (ca.40-90) provides important evidence on Greek and Roman knowledge of medicinal plants. Dioscorides is famous for writing a five volume book in his native Greek (*De Materia Medica* — in the Latin translation) that is one of the most influential herbal books in history. In fact, it remained in use until about CE 1600. Approximately 1300-1400 different plant species were known under Roman reign.

Mediaeval Botany

The Persian biologist Abu ?anifa Dinawari (828-896) is considered the founder of Arabic botany for his *Book of Plants*, in which he described at least 637 plants and discussed plant development from germination to death, describing the phases of plant growth and the production of flowers and fruit.

Theophrastus's *Historia Plantarum* served as a reference point in botany for many centuries, and was further developed around 1200 by Giovanni Bodeo da Stapelio, who added a *commentarius* and drawings: see Historia Plantarum — *Selected pages of a 17th century edition of the 1200 version (in Italian).*

In the early 13th century, the Andalusian-Arabian biologist Abu al-Abbas al-Nabati developed an early scientific method for botany, introducing empirical and experimental techniques in the testing, description and identification of numerous materia medica, and separating unverified reports from those supported by actual tests and observations. His student Ibn al-Baitar (d. 1248) wrote a pharmaceutical encyclopedia describing 1,400 plants, foods, and drugs, 300 of which were his own original discoveries. A Latin translation of his work was useful to European biologists and pharmacists in the 18th and 19th centuries.

German physician Leonhart Fuchs (1501-1566) was one of the three founding fathers of botany, along with Otto Brunfels (1489-1534) and Hieronymus Bock (1498-1554) (also called Hieronymus Tragus).

Valerius Cordus (1515-1554) authored one of the greatest pharmacopoeias and one of the most celebrated herbals in history, *Dispensatorium* (1546). As early as the 16th century, the Italian Ulisse Aldrovandi was scientifically researching plants. In 1665, using an early microscope, Robert Hooke discovered cells in cork, and a short time later in living plant tissue. The Germans Jacob Theodor Klein and Leonhart Fuchs, the Swiss Conrad von Gesner, and the British author Nicholas Culpeper published herbals that gave information on the medicinal uses of plants.

During the 18th century systems of classification became deliberately artificial and served only for the purpose of identification. These classifications are comparable to diagnostic keys, where taxa are artificially grouped in pairs by few, easily recognisable characters. The sequence of the taxa in keys is often totally unrelated to their natural or phyletic groupings. In the 18th century an increasing number of new plants had arrived in Europe, from newly discovered countries and the European colonies worldwide, and a larger amount of plants became available for study.

In 1754 Carl von Linné (Carl Linnaeus) divided the plant Kingdom into 25 classes. One, the *Cryptogamia*, included all the plants with concealed reproductive parts (algae, fungi, mosses and liverworts and ferns).

The increased knowledge on anatomy, morphology and life cycles, lead to the realization that there were more natural affinities between plants, than the sexual system of Linnaeus indicated. Adanson (1763), Jussieu (1789), and Candolle (1819) all proposed various alternative natural systems that were widely followed. The ideas of natural selection as a mechanism for evolution required adaptations to the Candollean system, which started the studies on evolutionary relationships and phylogenetic classifications of plants.

A considerable amount of new knowledge today is being generated from studying model plants like *Arabidopsis thaliana*. This weedy species in the mustard family was one of the first plants to have its genome sequenced. The sequencing of the rice (*Oryza sativa*) genome, its relatively small genome, and a large international research community have made rice an important cereal/grass/monocot model. Another grass species, *Brachypodium distachyon* is also emerging as an experimental model for understanding the genetic, cellular and molecular biology of temperate grasses. Other commercially-important staple foods like wheat, maize, barley, rye, pearl millet and soybean are also having their genomes sequenced. Some of these are challenging to sequence because they have more than two haploid (n) sets of chromosomes, a condition known as polyploidy, common in the plant kingdom. *Chlamydomonas reinhardtii* (a single-celled, green alga) is another plant model organism that has been extensively studied and provided important insights into cell biology.

In 1998 the Angiosperm Phylogeny Group published a phylogeny of flowering plants based on an analysis of DNA sequences from most families of flowering plants. As a result of this work, major questions such as which families represent the earliest branches in the genealogy of angiosperms are now understood. Investigating how plant species are related to each other allows botanists to better understand the process of evolution in plants.

Genetic Engineering

Genetic engineering, recombinant DNA technology, genetic modification/manipulation (GM) and gene splicing are terms that apply to the direct manipulation of an organism's genes. Genetic engineering is different from traditional breeding, where the organism's genes are manipulated indirectly. Genetic engineering uses the techniques of molecular cloning and transformation to alter the structure and characteristics of genes directly. Genetic engineering techniques have found some successes in numerous applications. Some examples are in improving crop technology, the manufacture of synthetic human insulin through the use of modified bacteria, the manufacture of erythropoietin in hamster ovary cells, and the production of new types of experimental mice such as the oncomouse (cancer mouse) for research.

The term 'genetic engineering' was coined in Jack Williamson's science fiction novel *Dragon's Island*, published in 1951, one year before DNA's role in heredity was confirmed in 1952 by Alfred Hershey and Martha Chase and two years before James Watson and Francis Crick showed that DNA has a double-helix structure.

The DNA-protein system is an ingeniously simple and extremely powerful solution for creating all kinds of biological properties and structures. Just by varying the sequence of code words in the DNA, innumerable variations of proteins with very disparate properties can be obtained, sufficient to generate the enormous variety of biological life.

There are a number of ways through which genetic engineering is accomplished. Essentially, the process has five main steps:

1. Isolation of the genes of interest.
2. Insertion of the genes into a transfer vector.
3. Transfer of the vector to the organism to be modified.
4. Transformation of the cells of the organism.
5. Selection of the genetically modified organism (GMO) from those that have not been successfully modified.

Isolation is achieved by identifying the gene of interest that the scientist wishes to insert into the organism, usually using existing knowledge of the various functions of genes. DNA information can be obtained from cDNA or gDNA libraries, and amplified using PCR techniques. If necessary, i.e. for insertion of eukaryotic genomic DNA into prokaryotes, further modification may be carried out such as removal of introns or ligating prokaryotic promoters.

Insertion of a gene into a vector such as a plasmid can be done once the gene of interest is isolated. Other vectors can also be used, such as viral vectors, bacterial conjugation, liposomes, or even direct insertion using a gene gun. Restriction enzymes and ligases are of great use in this crucial step if it is being inserted into prokaryotic or viral vectors. Daniel Nathans, Werner Arber and Hamilton Smith received the 1978 Nobel Prize in Physiology or Medicine for their isolation of restriction endonucleases.

Once the vector is obtained, it can be used to *transform* the *target organism*. Depending on the vector used, it can be complex or simple. For example, using raw DNA with gene guns is a fairly straightforward process but with low success rates, where the DNA is coated with molecules such as gold and fired directly into a cell. Other more complex methods, such as bacterial transformation or using viruses as vectors have higher success rates.

After transformation, the GMO can be selected from those that have failed to take up the vector in various ways. One method is screening with DNA probes that can stick to the gene of interest that was supposed to have been transplanted. Another is to package genes conferring resistance to certain chemicals such as antibiotics or herbicides into the vector. This chemical is then applied ensuring that only those cells that have taken up the vector will survive.

Applications

Molecular biologists have discovered many enzymes which change the structure of DNA in living organisms. Some of these enzymes can cut and join strands of DNA. Using such enzymes, scientists learned to cut specific genes from DNA and to build customized DNA using these genes. They also learned about vectors, strands of DNA such as viruses, which can infect a cell and insert themselves into its DNA.

The first genetically engineered medicine was synthetic human insulin, approved by the United States Food and Drug Administration in 1982. Another early application of genetic engineering was to create human growth hormone as replacement for a compound that was previously extracted from human cadavers. In 1987 the FDA approved the first genetically engineered vaccine for humans, for hepatitis B. Since these early uses of the technology in medicine, the use of GM has gradually expanded to supply a number of other drugs and vaccines.

One of the best-known applications of genetic engineering is the creation of GMOs for food use (genetically modified foods); such foods resist insect pests, bacterial or fungal infection, resist herbicides to improve yield, have longer freshness than otherwise, or have superior nutritional value.

In materials science, a genetically modified virus has been used to construct a more environment friendly lithium-ion battery.

A new type of slowly growing artform is being established via gene engineering and manipulation. Bioart, an artistic form, uses gene engineering to create new art forms that both educate the public about genetics and create living artforms.

Although there has been a revolution in the biological sciences in the past twenty years, there is still a great deal that remains to be discovered. The completion of the sequencing of the human genome, as well as the genomes of most agriculturally and scientifically important animals and plants, has increased the possibilities of genetic research immeasurably. Expedient and inexpensive access to comprehensive genetic data has become a reality with billions of sequenced nucleotides already online and annotated.

Knockout Mice

Loss of function experiments, such as in a gene knockout experiment, in which an organism is engineered to lack the activity of one or more genes. This allows the experimenter to analyze the defects caused by this mutation, and can be considerably useful in unearthing the function of a gene. It is used especially frequently in developmental biology. A knockout experiment involves the creation and manipulation of a DNA construct *in vitro*, which, in a simple knockout, consists of a copy of the desired gene, which has been slightly altered such as to cripple its function. The construct is then taken up by embryonic stem cells, wherein the engineered copy of the gene replaces the organism's own gene. These stem cells are injected into blastocysts, which are implanted into surrogate mothers. Another method, useful in organisms such as Drosophila (fruitfly), is to induce mutations in a large population and then screen the progeny for the desired mutation. A similar process can be used in both plants and prokaryotes.

Gain of function experiments, the logical counterpart of knockouts. These are sometimes performed in conjunction with knockout experiments to more finely establish the function of the desired gene. The process is much the same as that in knockout engineering, except that the construct is designed to increase the function of the gene, usually by providing extra copies of the gene or inducing synthesis of the protein more frequently.

Tracking experiments, which seek to gain information about the localization and interaction of the desired protein. One way to do this is to replace the wild-type gene with a 'fusion' gene, which is a juxtaposition of the wild-type gene with a reporting element such as Green Fluorescent Protein (GFP) that will allow easy visualization of the products of the genetic modification. While this is a useful technique, the manipulation can destroy the function of the gene, creating secondary effects and possibly calling into question the results of the experiment. More sophisticated techniques are now in development that can track protein products without mitigating their function, such as the addition of small sequences that will serve as binding motifs to monoclonal antibodies.

Expression studies aim to discover where and when specific proteins are produced. In these experiments, the DNA sequence before the DNA that codes for a protein, known as a gene's promoter, is reintroduced into an organism with the protein coding region replaced by a reporter gene such as GFP or an enzyme that catalyzes the production of a dye. Thus the time and place where a particular protein is produced can be observed. Expression studies can be taken a step further by altering the promoter to find which pieces are crucial for the proper expression of the gene and are actually bound by transcription factor proteins; this process is known as promoter bashing.

Human Genetic Engineering

Human genetic engineering can be used to treat genetic disease, but there is a difference between treating the disease in an individual and changing the genome that gets passed down to that person's descendants (germ-line genetic engineering).

Human genetic engineering has the potential to change human beings' appearance, adaptability, intelligence, character, and behavior. It may potentially be used in creating more dramatic changes in humans. There are many unresolved ethical issues and concerns surrounding this technology, and it remains a controversial topic.

Forms

Genetic engineering can enable the transport of genes between unrelated (transgenesis) or related (cisgenesis) organisms that would otherwise be unable to occur naturally, due to differences in anatomy or the incorrespondence between the DNA structures. This form of genetic engineering can produce unpredictable results to the genome of the organisms, and can be related to those mutation processes.

Advantages

The modification of the DNA structures of agricultural crops can increase the growth rates and even resistance to different diseases caused by pathogens and parasites. This is extremely beneficial as it can greatly increase the production of food sources with the usage of fewer resources that would be required to host the world's growing populations. These modified crops would also reduce the usage of chemicals, such as fertilizers and pesticides, and therefore decrease the severity and frequency of the damages produced by these chemical pollution. Domesticated animals can undergo the same mechanism. Genetic engineering can also increase the genetic diversity of species populations, especially those that are classified as being endangered. Increase in genetic diversity would enabled these organisms to evolve more efficiently that would allow better adaptation to the ecosystems they inhabit. It would also reduce the vulnerability of certain diseases produced by pathogens, as well as decrease the risk of inbreeding that would produce infertile youths. Genetic engineering can be performed to increase to the efficiency of the ecosystem services provided by the other organisms. For example, the modification of a tree's genes could perhaps increase the root systems of these organisms reduce the damage produced by flood phenomena through flood mitigation.

Nut (Fruit)

Nut is a hard shelled fruit of some plants that has an indehiscent seed. While a wide variety of dried seeds and fruits are called nuts in English, only a certain number of them are considered by biologists to be *true nuts.* Nuts are an important source of nutrients for both humans and wildlife.

Nuts are a composite of the seed and the fruit, where the fruit does not open to release the seed. Most seeds come from fruits, and the seeds are free of the fruit, unlike nuts like hazelnuts, hickories, chestnuts and acorns, which have a stony fruit wall and originate from a compound ovary. Culinary usage of the term is less restrictive, and some nuts as defined in food preparation, like pistachios and Brazil nuts, are not nuts in a biological sense. Everyday common usage of the term often refers to any hard walled, edible kernel, as a nut.

Botanical Definition

A nut in botany is a simple dry fruit with one seed (rarely two) in which the ovary wall becomes very hard (stony or woody) at maturity, and where the seed remains attached or fused with the ovary wall. Most nuts come from the pistils with *inferior* ovaries (see flower) and all are *indehiscent* (not opening at maturity). True nuts are produced, for example, by some plant families of the order Fagales.

- Order Fagales
- Family Fagaceae:
  - Chestnut (*Castanea*)
  - Beech (*Fagus*)
  - Oak (*Quercus*)
  - Stone-oak, Tanoak (*Lithocarpus*)
  - Family Betulaceae
  - Alder (*Alnus*)
  - Hazel, Filbert (*Corylus*)
  - Hornbeam

Culinary Definition and Uses

A nut in cuisine is a much less restrictive category than a nut in botany, as the term is applied to many seeds that are not botanically true nuts. Any large, oily kernel found within a shell and used in food may be regarded as a nut. Pistachios are seeds enclosed in a tough fruit, which do not split open enough to release the seeds.

The grouping of many similar dry seeds and fruits under the single generic name 'nut' is not followed in many other languages, which have only individual names for each type. Because nuts generally have a high oil content, they are a highly prized food and energy source. A large number of seeds are edible by humans and used in cooking, eaten raw, sprouted, or roasted as a snack food, or pressed for oil that is used in cookery and cosmetics. Nuts (or seeds generally) are also a significant source of nutrition for wildlife. This is particularly true in temperate climates where animals such as jays and squirrels store acorns and other nuts during the autumn to keep them from starving during the late autumn, all of winter, and early spring.

Nuts used for food, whether true nut or not, are among the most common food allergens.

Some fruits and seeds that do not meet the botanical definition but are nuts in the culinary sense:

- Almonds and walnuts are the edible seeds of drupe fruits – the leathery flesh' is removed at harvest.
- Brazil nut is the seed from a capsule.
- Candlenut (used for oil) is a seed.
- Cashew nut is a seed.
- Coconut is a dry, fibrous drupe.
- Gevuinanut
- Horse-chestnut is an inedible capsule.
- Macadamia nut is a creamy white kernel (Macadamia integrifolia).
- Malabar chestnut.
- Mongongo.
- Peanut is a seed. It is actually not a nut at all, but a legume.
- Pine nut is the seed of several species of pine (coniferous trees).
- Pistachio nut is the seed of a thin-shelled drupe.

Several epidemiological studies have revealed that people who consume nuts regularly are less likely to suffer from coronary heart disease. Recent clinical trials have found that consumption of various nuts such as almonds and walnuts can lower serum LDL cholesterol concentrations. Although nuts contain various substances thought to possess cardioprotective effects, scientists believe that their Omega 3 fatty acid profile is at least in part responsible for the hypolipidemic response observed in clinical trials.

In addition to possessing cardioprotective effects, nuts generally have a very low glycemic index (GI). Consequently, dietitians frequently recommend nuts be included in diets prescribed for patients with insulin resistance problems such as diabetes mellitus type 2.

One study found that people who eat nuts live two to three years longer than those who do not. However, this may be because people who eat nuts tend to eat less junk food.

Nuts contain the all important fatty acids, linoleic and linolenic acids, which are critical for growth, physical and mental development, healthy hair and skin, blood pressure control, immunological responses and blood clotting. In addition, the fats in nuts for the most part are unsaturated fats, particularly monounsaturated fats. This type does not elevate blood cholesterol levels like saturated fats.

Furthermore nuts supply one of the best natural sources of vitamins E, F, and G (docopherol, an antioxidant) , and are rich in protein, folate, fibre, and essential minerals such as magnesium, phosphorus, potassium, copper, and selenium.

The nut of the horse-chestnut tree (*Aesculus* species, especially *Aesculus hippocastanum*), is called a *conker* in the British Isles. Conkers are inedible because they contain toxic glucoside aesculin. They are used in a popular children's game, known as *conkers*, where the nuts are threaded onto a strong cord and then each contestant attempts to break his opponent's conker by hitting it with his own. Horse chestnuts are also popular slingshot ammunition.

A related species, *Aesculus californica*, was eaten by the Native Americans of California during famines after the toxic constituents were leached out.

Lawn

A *lawn* is an area of recreational or amenity land planted with grass, and sometimes clover and other plants, which are maintained at a low, even height.

The specialised names turf, pitch, field or green may be used, depending on the sport and the locale.

Lawns are a standard feature of ornamental private and public gardens and landscapes in much of the world today. Lawns are created for aesthetic use in gardens, and for recreational use, including sports. They are typically planted near homes, often as part of gardens, and are also used in other ornamental landscapes and gardens.

Lawns are frequently a feature of public parks and other spaces. They form the playing surface for many outdoor sports, reducing erosion and dust as well as providing a cushion for players in sports such as Rugby, football, cricket, baseball, golf, tennis, bocce and stake.

Many different species of grass are used, often depending on the intended use of the lawn, with vigorous, coarse grasses used where active sports are played, and much finer, softer grasses on ornamental lawns, and partly on climate, with different grasses adapted to oceanic climates with cool summers, and tropical and continental climates with hot summers. It is also not uncommon to mix grass seeds. A 50/50 mixture of grass types can, for example, form a stronger lawn when one grass type does better in the warmer seasons and the other is more resistant to colder weather.

Before the invention of mowing machines in 1830, lawns were managed very differently. Lawns belonging to wealthy people were sometimes maintained by the labour-intensive methods of scything and shearing–in most cases, however, they were pasture land which was maintained through grazing by sheep or other livestock. Areas of grass grazed regularly by rabbits, horses or sheep over a long period often form a very low, tight sward similar to a modern lawn. This was the original meaning of the word 'lawn', and the term can still be found in place-names. Some forest areas where extensive grazing is practiced still have these semi-natural lawns. For example, in the New Forest, England, such grazed areas are common and are known as *lawns*, for example Balmer Lawn.

Lawns became popular in Europe from the Middle Ages onward. The early lawns were not always distinguishable from pasture fields. It is thought that the associations with pasture and the biblical connotations of this word made them attractive culturally. By contrast, they are little-known or used in this form in other traditions of gardening. In addition, the damp climate of maritime Western Europe made them easier to grow and manage than in other regions.

During Victorian times, as more plants were introduced into Britain and the influence of France and Italy became prevalent, lawns became smaller as borders were created and filled with plants, statues, sculptures, terraces and water features, which started encroaching onto the area covered by the lawn. In the United States, it was not until after the Civil War that lawns began to appear outside middle-class residences. Most people did not have the hired labour needed to cut a field of grass with scythes; average home owners either raised vegetables in their yards or left them alone. If weeds sprouted that was fine. Toward the end of the 19th century, suburbs appeared on the American scene, along with the sprinkler, greatly improved lawn mowers, new ideas about landscaping and a shorter working week.

Lawns do not have to be, and have not always been, made up of grass alone. Other plants for fine lawns in the right conditions are camomile and thyme. Some lawns, if grown in difficult conditions for grasses, become dominated by whatever weeds can survive there; these include clovers in dry conditions, and moss in damp shady conditions. In more recent times, especially in suburban residential areas, a lawn may refer to an area surrounding a home where some or all of the natural grass or sod has been removed and replaced with artificial turf, stones, mulch, or some other material determined by the homeowner to reduce maintenance and/or water consumption.

A number of criticisms of lawns are based on environmental grounds.

Many lawns are composed of a single species of plant, or of very few species, which reduces biodiversity, especially if the lawn covers a large area. In addition, they may be composed primarily of plants not local to the area, which can further decrease local biodiversity.

Lawns are sometimes cared for by using synthetic pesticides and other chemicals, which can be harmful to the environment, especially when misused.

Consequently, in Canada, for example, over 140 municipalities and the entire province of Quebec have now placed restrictions on the cosmetic use of synthetic lawn pesticides as a result of health and environmental concerns The Ontario provincial government promised on September 24, 2007 to also implement a province-wide ban on the cosmetic use of lawn pesticides, for protecting the public. Medical and environmental groups support such a ban. On April 22, 2008, the Provincial Government of Ontario announced that it will pass legislation that will prohibit, province-wide, the cosmetic use and sale of lawn and garden pesticides. The Ontario legislation would also echo Massachusetts law requiring pesticide manufacturers to reduce the toxins they use in production The Province of Prince Edward Island is also considering such legislation. On April 3, 2008, the Canadian Cancer Society released opinion poll results conducted by Ipsos Reid, which established that a clear majority of residents in the provinces of British Columbia and Saskatchewan want province-wide cosmetic lawn pesticide bans, and that the majority of respondents believe that cosmetic pesticides are a threat to their health.

Sweden, Denmark, Norway, Kuwait and Belize have also placed restrictions on the use of the herbicide.

The use of pesticides and synthetic fertilizers, which require fossil fuels to be manufactured, has been shown to be detrimental to combating global warming, whereas organic techniques help reduce global warming.

Maintaining a green lawn sometimes requires large amounts of water. This was not a problem in temperate England where the concept of the lawn originated, as natural rainfall was sufficient to maintain a lawn's health. However the exporting of the lawn ideal to more arid regions of the world, such as the U.S. Southwest and Australia, has crimped already scarce water resources in such areas, requiring larger, more environmentally invasive water supply systems. Grass typically goes dormant during cold, winter months, and turns brown during hot, dry summer months, thereby reducing its demand for water. Many property owners consider this 'dead' appearance unacceptable and therefore increase watering during the summer months. Grass can also recover quite well from a drought.

In the United States lawn heights are generally maintained by gasoline-powered lawnmowers, which contribute to urban smog during the summer months. The U.S. Environmental Protection Agency found that in some urban areas, up to 5 per cent of smog was due to pre-1997 small gasoline engines such as are typically used on lawnmowers. Since 1997, the EPA has mandated emissions controls on newer engines in an effort to reduce smog.

However, using ecological techniques, the impact of lawns can sometimes be reduced. Such methods include the use of local grasses, proper mowing techniques, leaving grass clippings in place, integrated pest management, organic fertilizers, and introducing a variety of plants to the lawn.

In addition to the environmental criticisms, some gardeners question the aesthetic value of lawns.

One positive benefit of a healthy lawn is that of a filter for contaminants and to prevent run-off and erosion of bare dirt. Highway construction projects in the United States now routinely include replanting grasses on disturbed soils for this purpose, although they are not maintained as lawns. It is important to note that a healthy lawn does not necessarily mean that synthetic pesticides need to be used, as organic solutions exist.

It was not until the Tudor and Elizabethan times that the garden and the lawn became a place to be loved and admired. Created as walkways and for play areas, the lawns were not as we envisage them today. They were made up of meadow plants, such as camomile, a particular favourite. In the early 1600s the Jacobean epoch of gardening began. It was during this period that the closely-cut 'English' lawn was born. By the end of this period, the English lawn was the envy of even the French; it was also seen as a symbol of status by the gentry. In the early 1700s, gardening fashion went through a further change. William Kent and the age of Capability Brown were in progress, and the open 'English' style of parkland was seen across Britain and Ireland. Lawns seemed to flow from the garden into the outer landscape.

Establishment

Lawns are established through one of three methods:

1. planting of seeds across the area, which germinate and grown as grass;

2. planting of runners (small grass plants) which then propagate across the area by natural spread;
3. laying of turf on the area, essentially transplating a lawn from another location (usually a *turf farm*).

Maintenance

Maintaining a rough lawn requires only occasional cutting with a suitable machine, or grazing by animals. There is often heavy social pressure to mow one's lawn regularly and to keep up with the Joneses.

Maintaining higher quality lawns may require special maintenance procedures:

- Mowing regularly with a sharp blade at an even height.
- Not mowing when lawn is wet.
- Not removing more than 30 per cent to 40 per cent of the plant tissue.
- Alternating the direction of cut from previous mowing.
- Scarifying and raking, to remove dead grass and prevent tufting.
- Rolling, (to encourage tillering (branching of grass plants) and to level the ground).
- Top dressing with sand, soil or other material.
- Spiking or aeration (to relieve compaction of the soil).
- Additional watering.
- Fertilizing application.
- Organic or synthetic pesticide application.

Seasonal lawn care will vary to some extent depending on the climate zone and type of grass that is grown, whether cool season or warm season varieties. In general, however, there are recognized steps in lawn care that should be observed in any of these areas.

Spring or early summer is the time to seed, sod, or sprig a yard, when the ground is warmer. For a new lawn, adding a fresh load of topsoil to the ground is beneficial. Seeding the lawn is the least expensive way to plant, but it takes longer for the lawn to grow and usually needs daily watering, or the freshly-sprouted grass will die. Sodding is more expensive, but it will provide an almost instant lawn that can be planted in most climate zones in any season. Hydroseeding is a relatively quick and inexpensive method of planting. A nitrogen-based, slow-release fertilizer may be applied, when needed. Pesticides, which is an umbrella term that include herbicides, insecticides and fungicides, may be considered for use on lawns when required, and where legal. In Canada, over 130 municipalities and the province of Quebec prohibit the use of synthetic lawn pesticides. Although synthetic pesticides exist, organic solutions are increasingly being used. For example, corn gluten meal controls weed seeds by releasing an organic dipeptide into the soil and inhibiting root formation of germinating weed seeds. An application of beneficial nematodes can be used to combat grubs.

Summer lawn care requires raising the lawn mower for cool season grass, and lowering it for warm season lawns. Lawns will require longer and more frequent watering, best done in early morning to encourage a stronger root system. This is also the time to apply an all-purpose fertilizer. During the hot summer months, lawns may be susceptible to fungus disease. It's advisable to take a sod sample to a local landscape expert for testing and treating the yard, if necessary.

In the autumn, lawns can be mowed at a lower height and thatch buildup that occurs in warm season grasses should be removed, although lawn experts are divided in their opinions on this. This is also a good time to add a sandy loam and apply fertilizer, one that contains some type of wetting agent. Cool season lawns can be planted in autumn if there is adequate rainfall.

Lawn care in the winter is minimal, requiring only light feedings of organic material, such as green-waste compost, and minerals to encourage earthworms and beneficial microbes.

Types of Lawngrass

There are thousands of varieties of lawngrass, each adapted to specific conditions of precipitation, temperature, and sun/shade tolerance. Breeders are constantly creating new and improved varieties of the base list of lawngrass species. The two basic categories are cool season grasses and warm season grasses.

Cool season grasses start growth at 5 °C, and grow at their fastest rate when temperatures are between 10-25 °C, in climates that have relatively mild/cool summers, with two periods of rapid growth in the spring and autumn. They retain their colour well in extreme cold and typically grow very dense, carpetlike lawns with relatively little thatch.

- Bluegrass
- Bentgrass
- Ryegrasses
- Fescues

Warm season grasses only start growth at temperatures above 10°C, and grow fastest when temperatures are between 25°C and 35°C, with one long growth period over the spring and summer. They often go dormant in cooler months, turning shades of tan or brown. Many warm season grasses are quite drought tolerant, and can handle very high summer temperatures, although temperatures below -15°C can kill most southern ecotype warm season grasses. The northern varieties such as buffalograss and blue grama are hardy to -45°C.

- Zoysia grass
- Bermuda grass

- St. Augustine grass
- Bahia grass
- Centipede grass
- Carpet grass
- Buffalo grass
- Grama grass

Some people replace their lawns with ground creepers such as Creeping Jenny. But in fact, there are many alternatives to lawns including meadows, butterfly gardens, rain gardens, and kitchen gardens. Planting trees and shrubs in naturalistic arrangements can help restore habitat for birds and wildlife. But where people want a lawn-like area, they can use regionally appropriate species of low growing or mowable plants in lawn areas such as clover, creeping Charley, or sedum instead of high-maintenance turf grass.

Introduced Species

An introduced, alien, exotic, non-indigenous, or non-native species, or simply an introduction, is a species living outside its native distributional range, which has arrived there by human activity, either deliberate or accidental. Some introduced species are damaging to the ecosystem they are introduced into, others negatively affect agriculture and other human uses of natural resources, or impact on the health of animals and humans. A list of introduced species is given in a separate article. Introduced species and their effects on natural environments is a controversial subject and one that has gained much scrutiny by scientists, governments, farmers and others.

The terminology associated with introduced species is presently in flux for a variety of reasons. Other terms that are used sometimes interchangeably (having the same or similar meanings) with *introduced* are *acclimatized*, *adventive*, *naturalized*, *immigrant*, and *xenobiotic*. Nonetheless, distinctions can and should be made between some of these terms.

In the broadest and most widely used sense, an introduced species is synonymous with *non-native* and therefore applies as well to most garden and farm organisms; these adequately fit the basic definition given above. However, some sources add to that basic definition: "...and are now reproducing in the wild", which removes from consideration as *introduced* all of those species raised or grown in gardens or farms that do not survive without tending by people. With respect to plants, these latter are in this case defined as either *ornamental* or *cultivated* plants.

The following definition from the United States Environmental Protection Agency, although perhaps lacking ecological sophistication, is more typical: *introduced species* are .."[s]pecies that have become able to survive and reproduce outside the habitats where they evolved or spread naturally". However, introduction of a species outside its native range is often all that is required to be qualified as an 'introduced species' such that one can distinguish between introduced species that may only occur in cultivation, under domestication or captivity whereas other become established outside their native range and reproduce without human assistance. Such species might be termed 'naturalized', 'established', 'wild non-native species', or 'invasive'. The transition from introduction, to establishment and invasion has been described by in the context of plants. Introduced species are essentially 'non-native' species. Invasive species are those introduced species that spread-widely or quickly, and cause harm, be that to the environment, human health, other valued resources or the economy. There have been calls from scientists to consider a species 'invasive' only in terms of their spread and reproduction rather than the harm they may cause.

An invasive species is one that has been introduced and become a pest in its new location, spreading (invading) by natural means. The term is used to imply both a sense of urgency and actual or potential harm. For example, U.S. Executive Order 13112 (1999) defines 'invasive species' as "an alien species whose introduction does or is likely to cause economic or environmental harm or harm to human health"

Although some argue that 'invasive' is a loaded word and harm is difficult to define, the fact of the matter is that organisms have and continue to be introduced to areas where they are not native, sometimes with, usually without, much regard to the harm that could result.

From a regulatory perspective, it is neither desirable nor practical to simply list as undesirable or outright ban all non-native species (although the State of Hawaii has adopted an approach that comes close to this). Regulations require a definitional distinction between non-natives that are deemed especially onerous and all others. Introduced *pest species* that are *officially listed* as invasive, best fit the definition of an *invasive species.*

Nature of Introductions

By definition, a species is considered 'introduced' when its transport into an area outside of its native range is human mediated. Introductions by humans can be described as either intentional or accidental. Intentional introductions have been motivated by individuals or groups who believe that the newly introduced species will be in some way beneficial to humans in its new location. Unintentional or accidental introductions are most often a byproduct of human movements, and are thus unbound to human motivations. Subsequent range expansion of introduced species may or may not involve human activity.

Intentional Introductions

Species that humans intentionally transport to new regions can subsequently become successfully established in two ways. In the first case, organisms are purposely released for establishment in the wild. It is sometimes difficult to predict whether a species will become established upon release, and if not initially successful, humans have made repeated introductions to improve the probability that the species will survive and eventually reproduce in the wild. In these cases it is clear that the introduction is directly facilitated by human desires.

In the second case, species intentionally transported into a new region may escape from captive or cultivated populations and subsequently establish independent breeding populations. Escaped organisms are included in this category because their initial transport to a new region is human motivated.

Perhaps the most common motivation for introducing a species into a new place is that of economic gain. Examples of species introduced for the purposes of benefiting agriculture, aquaculture or other economic activities are widespread Eurasian carp was first introduced to the United States as a potential food source. The apple snail was released in Southeast Asia with the intent that it be used as a protein source, and subsequently to places like Hawaii to establish a food industry. In Alaska, foxes were introduced to many islands to create new populations for the fur trade. The timber industry promoted the introduction of Monterey Pine (*Pinus radiata*) from California to Australia and New Zealand as a commercial timber crop. These examples represent only a small subsample of species that have been moved by humans for economic interests.

Introductions have also been important in supporting recreation activities or otherwise increasing human enjoyment. Numerous fish and game animals have been introduced for the purposes of sport fishing and hunting. The introduced amphibian (*Ambystoma tigrinum*) that threatens the endemic California salamander (*Ambystoma californiense*) was introduced to California as a source of bait for fishermen. Pet animals have also been frequently transported into new areas by humans, and their escapes have resulted in several successful introductions, such as those of feral cats and parrots.

Many plants have been introduced with the intent of aesthetically improving public recreation areas or private properties. The introduced Norway Maple for example occupies a prominent status in many of Canada's parks. The transport of ornamental plants for landscaping use has and continues to be a source of many introductions. Some of these species have escaped horticultural control and become invasive. Notable examples include water hyacinth, salt cedar, and purple loosestrife.

In other cases, species have been translocated for reasons of "cultural nostalgia," which refers to instances in which humans who have migrated to new regions have intentionally brought with them familiar organisms. Famous examples include the introduction of starlings to North America by Englishman Eugene Schieffelin, a lover of the works of Shakespeare, who, it is rumoured, wanted to introduce all of the birds mentioned in Shakespeare's plays into the United States. He deliberately released eighty starlings into Central Park in New York City in 1890, and another forty in 1891. Yet another prominent example is the introduction of the European rabbit to Australia by one Thomas Austin, a British landowner who had the rabbits released on his estate in Victoria because he missed hunting them. A more recent example is the introduction of the wall lizard to North America by a Cincinnati boy, George Rau, in the 1950s after a family vacation to Italy.

Intentional introductions have also been undertaken with the aim of ameliorating environmental problems. A number of fast spreading plants such as Garlic Mustard and kudzu have been introduced as a means of erosion control. Other species have been introduced as biological control agents to control invasive species and involves the purposeful introduction of a natural enemy of the target species with the intention of reducing its numbers or controlling its spread.

A special case of introduction is the reintroduction of a species that has become locally endangered or extinct, done in the interests of conservation. Examples of successful reintroductions include wolves to Yellowstone National Park in the U.S., and the Red kite to parts of England and Scotland. Introductions or translocations of species have also been proposed in the interest of genetic conservation, which advocates the introduction of new individuals into genetically depauperate populations of endangered or threatened species.

The above examples highlight the intent of humans to introduce species as a means of incurring some benefit. While these benefits have in some cases been realized, introductions have also resulted in unforeseen costs, particularly when introduced species take on characteristics of invasive species.

Non-native species can become such a common part of an environment, culture, and even diet that little thought is given to their geographic origin. For example, soybeans, kiwi fruit, wheat and all livestock except the llama and the turkey are non-native species to North America. Collectively, non-native crops and livestock comprise 98 per cent of US food. These and other benefits from non-natives are so vast that, according to the Congressional Research Service, they probably exceed the costs.

Unintentional introductions occur when species are transported by human vectors. For example, three species of rat (the Black, Norway and Polynesian) have spread to most of the world as hitchhikers on ships. There are also numerous examples of marine organisms being transported in ballast water, one being the zebra mussel. Over 200 species have been introduced to the San Francisco Bay in this manner making it the most heavily invaded estuary in the world. Increasing rates of human travel are providing accelerating opportunities for species to be accidentally transported into areas in which they are not considered native. There is also the accidental release of the Africanized honey bees (AHB), known colloquially as 'killer bees' or Africanized bee to Brazil in 1957 and the Asian carps to the United States.

Introduced Plants and Algae

Many non-native plants have been introduced into new territories, initially as either ornamental plants or for erosion control, stock feed, or forestry. Whether an exotic will become invasive is seldom understood in the beginning, and many non-native ornamentals languish in the trade for years before suddenly naturalizing and becoming invasive.

Peaches, for example, originated in Persia, and have been carried to much of the populated world. Tomatoes are native to the Andes. Squash (pumpkins), maize, and tobacco are native to the Americas, but were introduced to the Old World. Many introduced species require continued human intervention to survive in the new environment. Others may become feral, but do not seriously compete with natives, but simply increase the biodiversity of the area.

Dandelions are also introduced species to North America.

A very troublesome marine species in southern Europe is the seaweed *Caulerpa taxifolia*. *Caulerpa* was first observed in the Mediterranean Sea in 1984, off the coast of Monaco. By 1997, it had covered some 50 km^2. It has a strong potential to overgrow natural biotopes, and represents a major risk for sublittoral ecosystems. The origin of the alga in the Mediterranean was thought to be either as a migration through the Suez Canal from the Red Sea, or as an accidental introduction from an aquarium.

Japanese knotweed grows profusely in many nations. Human beings introduced it into many places in the 19th century. It is a source of resveratrol, a dietary supplement.

One example of introducing an exotic animal was carried out by a lover of the works of Shakespeare, who wanted to introduce all of the birds mentioned in Shakespeare's plays into the United States. He deliberately released eighty starlings into Central Park in New York City in 1890, and another forty in 1891. The starling had been introduced previously into Ohio and had failed to survive.

Other examples of introduced animals include the gypsy moth in eastern North America, the zebra mussel and alewife in the Great Lakes, the Canada Goose and Gray Squirrel in Europe, the Muskrat in Europe and Asia, the Cane Toad and Red fox in Australia, Nutria in North America, Eurasia, and Africa, and the Common Brushtail Possum in New Zealand.

Invasive Exotic Diseases

History is rife with the spread of exotic diseases, such as the introduction of smallpox into the Americas, where it obliterated entire Native American civilizations before they were ever even seen by Europeans.

Problematic exotic disease introductions in the past century or so include the chestnut blight which has virtually extinguished the American chestnut, and Dutch elm disease, which has severely damaged the American elm.

Most Commonly Introduced Species

Some species, such as the Brown Rat, House Sparrow, Ring-necked Pheasant and European Starling, have been introduced very widely. In addition there are some agricultural and pet species that frequently become feral; these include rabbits, dogs, goats, fish, pigs and cats.

Perhaps the best place to study problems associated with introduced species is on islands. Depending upon the isolation (how far an island is located from continental biotas), native island biological communities may be poorly adapted to the threat posed by exotic introductions. Often this can mean that no natural predator of an introduced species is present, and the non-native spreads uncontrollably into open or occupied niche.

An additional problem is that birds native to small islands may have become flightless because of the absence of predators prior to introductions, and cannot readily escape danger. The tendency of rails in particular to evolve flightless forms on islands has led to the disproportionate number of extinctions in that family.

The field of island restoration has developed as a field of conservation biology and ecological restoration, a great deal of which deals with the eradication of introduced species.

New Zealand

In New Zealand the largest commercial crop is *Pinus radiata*, the Monterey Pine from California, which grows better in New Zealand than in California. However, the pine forests are also occupied by deer from North America and Europe and by possums from Australia. All are exotic species and all have thrived in the New Zealand environment. The pines are seen as beneficial while the deer and possums are regarded as serious pests.

Common gorse, originally a hedge plant in Scotland, was introduced to New Zealand for the same purpose. Like the radiata pine, it has shown a favour to its new climate and is regarded as a noxious plant which threatens to obliterate native plants in much of the country and is hence routinely eradicated, though it can also provide a nursery environment for native plants to reestablish themselves.

Rabbits, introduced as a food source by sailors in the 1800s, have become a severe nuisance to farmers, notably in South Island. The myxomatosis virus was illegally imported and illegally released but it had little lasting effect upon the rabbit population other than to make it more resistant to the virus.

Rats, brought either by the first humans to arrive in New Zealand (the Maori) or by Europeans have had a devastating effect upon native birdlife, particularly as many New Zealand birds are flightless. Feral cats and dogs which were originally brought as pets are also known to kill large numbers of birds. A recent (2006) study in South Island has shown that even domestic cats with a ready supply of food from their owners may kill hundreds of birds in a year, including natives.

Sparrows, which were brought to control insects upon the introduced grain crops, have displaced native birds as have Rainbow Lorikeets and cockatoos (both from Australia) which fly free around areas west of Auckland City such as the Waitakere Ranges.

In much of the New Zealand the Australian black swan has effectively eliminated the existence of the previously introduced mute swan.

Two notable varieties of spiders have also been introduced: the white tail spider and the black widow spider. Both may have arrived inside shipments of fruit. Prior to this the only spider (and the only poisonous animal) dangerous to humans was the native katipo which is very similar to the black widow and which is known to successfully interbreed with the more aggressive North American variety.

Genetic Pollution

Purebred naturally evolved region specific wild species can be threatened with extinction in a big way through the process of genetic pollution i.e. uncontrolled hybridization, introgression and genetic swamping which leads to homogenization or replacement of local genotypes as a result of either a numerical and/or fitness advantage of introduced plant or animal. Nonnative species can bring about a form of extinction of native plants and animals by hybridization and introgression either through purposeful introduction by humans or through habitat modification, bringing previously isolated species into contact. These phenomena can be especially detrimental for rare species coming into contact with more abundant ones where the abundant ones can interbreed with them swamping the entire rarer gene pool creating hybrids thus driving the entire original purebred native stock to complete extinction. Attention has to be focussed on the extent of this under appreciated problem that is not always apparent from morphological (outward appearance) observations alone. Some degree of gene flow may be a normal, evolutionarily constructive process, and all constellations of genes and genotypes cannot be preserved however, hybridization with or without introgression may, nevertheless, threaten a rare species' existence.

Index